SNIPER
IN HELMAND

SNIPER
IN HELMAND

James Cartwright

Pen & Sword
MILITARY

First published in Great Britain in 2011 and
reprinted in this format in 2014 by
PEN & SWORD MILITARY
An imprint of
Pen & Sword Books Ltd
47 Church Street
Barnsley, South Yorkshire
S70 2AS

ISBN 978 1 47382 273 3

A CIP catalogue record for this book is
available from the British Library.

Printed and bound in England by
CPI Group (UK) Ltd, Croydon, CR0 4YY

Pen & Sword Books Ltd incorporates the imprints of Aviation, Atlas,
Family History, Fiction, Maritime, Military, Discovery, Politics, History,
Archaeology, Select, Wharncliffe Local History, Wharncliffe True Crime,
Military Classics, Wharncliffe Transport, Leo Cooper, The Praetorian Press,
Remember When, Seaforth Publishing and Frontline Publishing.

For a complete list of Pen & Sword titles please contact
PEN & SWORD BOOKS LIMITED
47 Church Street, Barnsley, South Yorkshire, S70 2AS, England
E-mail: enquiries@pen-and-sword.co.uk
Website: www.pen-and-sword.co.uk

Contents

Acknowledgements

I would firstly like to thank every single soldier who fought alongside me during Operation HERRICK 6 and watched my back as I watched theirs. This tour was not conducted by one man but by a group of highly trained professional soldiers. Also I would like to thank all the officers and senior NCOs under whose command I fought for their excellence in leading me and the other soldiers.

I also want to extend a warm thanks to everyone who was involved in my treatment for Post Traumatic Stress Disorder. Without your help my life would have gone in a very different direction, and it was also out of this treatment that this book was born.

Another person I feel deserves a big thank you is Phil Dedman. Thank you, Phil for working very closely on this project with me, and for being such a good friend not only to me, but also to my family. Without you, none of this would have been possible.

I also thank Ross Kemp and everyone behind the tour magazine for helping me put together my memories in the correct order and reminding me of events I had forgotten.

A big thank you goes to Pen & Sword for putting this book together and for all of their help and support.

My appreciation goes out to everyone who gave me copies of their photographs. I always feel that this form of media is best for remembering. I have tried to get in touch with everyone whose photographs I have used in this book. However, there maybe some outstanding so please accept this acknowledgment as my thanks.

Of course not forgetting the families of the nine 1st Battalion Royal Anglian Regiment soldiers who did not come home. My heart goes out to you and my thoughts are with you and them every year on 11 November at 11.00.

Finally, I give massive thanks to all my family for supporting me during the difficult readjustment to normal life and, in particular, to Annie for putting up with my mood swings.

James Cartwright

Foreword

by

Andy McNab

The British army has never been better trained, equipped and prepared for conflict, but that doesn't stop the reality of a tour of duty being every bit as dangerous as it ever was. Conflict hasn't stopped taking its toll both emotionally and physically. James Cartwright has experienced one of the most hostile and dangerous areas of conflict of the present war. The work of snipers is crucial to so many current military operations. What he successfully conveys in *Sniper in Helmand* is the real feeling of being in a war zone. He tells it how it is to the reader – allowing them to experience the tactical decisions, pressures, acts of courage and of sacrifice that serving men and women go through each and every day.

Like me, James Cartwright started his army career as a boy soldier. We passed through many of the same establishments and I'm sure got bawled at by many similar RSMs along the way! We have both experienced the harsh reality of war zones and come home battle scarred emotionally and physically. Like him, I'd like to pay tribute to the men and women out there in the various war zones, the families left at home and also the many professionals who play such a vital role in the emotional and physical recovery.

Prologue

As the convoy came up the road, Deano was on top cover, standing up in a hatch in the roof of the Viking vehicle in which he and Teddy were travelling. Just behind him, strapped to the roof, were jerrycans of fuel and other items of kit. At that point a Taliban fighter launched an RPG from a nearby rooftop, scoring a direct hit on the roof of the vehicle, detonating on one of the jerrycans and causing a huge fireball that totally engulfed Deano in burning fuel. He dropped down back through the hatch of the vehicle, desperately trying to put out the flames and ripping off his helmet and body armour. Teddy meanwhile placed his hand on the rear door handle, readying himself to open it, but could clearly hear the sound of rounds literally pinging off the door on the outside. The Taliban had learned where our doors were and created a choice for those inside – either stay inside and burn to death or open the doors and be riddled with bullets.

At this point Deano jumped back up into the hatch of the vehicle, with no helmet or any body armour, and began to return fire with his SA80 rifle. At the same time, there was a short lull in the bullets pinging off the back door, so Teddy threw it open and, armed only with his 9mm pistol, leapt out and headed for a nearby an alleyway. There was deafening noise and dust all around him as bullets rained down and RPGs flew in from all directions. As he scrambled into the alleyway he came face to face with a Taliban fighter, shooting rounds into the air and screaming '*Allahu Akbar*!.' Teddy shot him dead on the spot before turning his attention back to the Viking. Realising that there was no movement from it, he ran back to the vehicle where he found Deano lying there unconscious inside, having been knocked out by the blast of another RPG hitting the roof.

Deano was in a mess. Severely burned from the blast and injured by shrapnel, he was losing blood and rapidly losing consciousness. He needed emergency medical treatment and quickly, as he was in a really bad way. Teddy clambered into the vehicle and dragged him out of the vehicle, all the while under fire from RPGs and automatic weapons, and slung him over his shoulder. Somehow he succeeded in reaching another Viking, throwing open the doors and heaving Deano inside. There was no room for himself so he had no choice but to run back another 50 or 60 metres, still under heavy fire, to another vehicle in which he took cover in the back.

All the while the fire support teams were bringing fire down on the enemy, but it was a relatively built-up town with high buildings all around which made manoeuvring almost impossible. The convoy was still under very heavy fire as it drove out of Sangin.

Glossary of Military Terms

2IC	Second-in-command
.338	L115A2 .338 calibre long range sniper rifle
AK-47	Soviet origin 7.62mm x 39 calibre assault rifle
ANA	Afghan National Army
ANP	Afghan National Police
CLU	Command Launcher Unit – for Javelin missile
CO	Commanding Officer
CQMS	Company Quartermaster Sergeant
CSM	Company Sergeant Major
CVR-T	Combat Vehicle Reconnaissance – Tracked
CWS	Common Weapon Sight – used with L85A2
DC	District Centre
Dragunov	Soviet origin 7.62mm x 54 calibre sniper rifle
F-15 Eagle	All-weather fighter
FAC	Forward air controller
FFD	First field dressing
FOB	Forward operating base
FSG	Fire support group
FST	Fire support team
FUP	Forming up point
GPMG	General purpose machine gun
HE	High explosive
ITC	Infantry Training Centre

GLOSSARY OF MILITARY TERMS

JDAM	Joint Defence Attack Munition
JTAC	Joint Terminal Air Controller
L96	L96A1 7.62mm x 51 NATO calibre sniper rifle
LMG	Light machine gun
LUP	Lying up place
MFC	Mortar fire controller
Minimi	L110A1 5.56mm x 45 NATO calibre belt-fed LMG
MOGs	Mobile operation groups
MRE	Meals ready to eat
MT	Motor transport
NCO	Non-Commissioned Officer
OC	Officer Commanding
OMLT	Operational Mentoring Liaison Team
OP	Observation Post
OPTAG	Operational Training Advisory Group
Orbat	Order of Battle
Pinzgauer	Light 4x4 or 6x6 vehicle
PRR	Personal role radio
Puritabs	Water purification tablets
PVCP	Permanent vehicle checkpoint
QRF	Quick reaction force
RPD	Russian or Chinese 7.62mm general purpose machine gun
RPG	Rocket propelled grenade
R & R	Rest and recuperation
RSM	Regimental Sergeant Major
RSOI	Reception, Staging & Onwards Integration
SA80	British 5.56mm x 45 NATO calibre assault rifle – official designation L85A2
SF	Special Forces
Sitrep	Situation Report

SPG-9	Russian 73mm tripod-mounted recoilless gun
SUSAT	Sight Unit Small Arms Trilux – used with L85A2
UGL	L17A2 underbarrel 40mm grenade launcher – fitted to L85A2
Viking BvS10	Armoured all terrain vehicle
Wadi	Permanently dried-up river bed
WMIK	Weapons Mounted Installation Kit
WO2	Warrant Officer Class 2

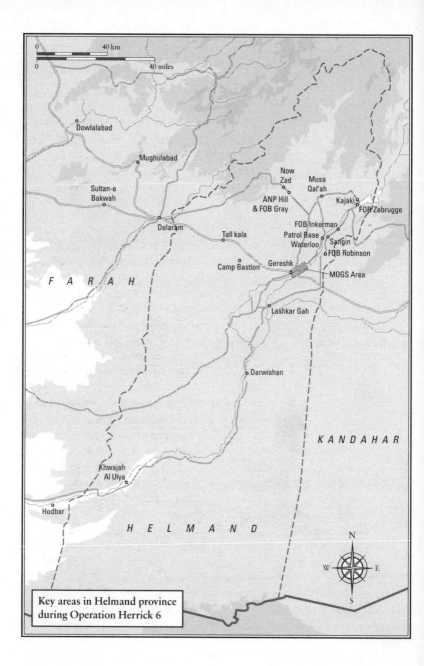

Key areas in Helmand province
during Operation Herrick 6

CHAPTER 1

The Beginning

There was never really any doubt that I would join the Army in some form or other. My father served in the Royal Navy seeing action in the Falklands War, and my two grandfathers served in the RAF and the Royal Army Service Corps during the 1950s. When you are bought up with this kind of heritage, and hear the stories that surround these experiences, I guess it was simply in the blood. My father and maternal grandfather were both marksmen and in due course I would follow in their footsteps, achieving marksman status in all of my annual personal weapons tests and ultimately becoming second-in-command of a sniper section.

At the age of sixteen, I attempted to join the Royal Marines. In hindsight this was far too early as my body had simply not developed sufficiently to cope with the physical standards required. However, I was close and completed the assessment tests satisfactorily apart from one that required you to lift your own body weight in the form of three overhand pull-ups immediately after a gruelling non-stop session in the gymnasium. I would have been able to pass it a few years later, but at that time I could not quite manage it and thus failed.

Soon afterwards, I telephoned the Army recruitment office in Reading, where I lived with my father at the time, to book an appointment to speak with the recruiting sergeant there. As I entered his office, I felt at ease and generally comfortable in myself. The sergeant himself was tall and amusing, and was in the Royal Gloucestershire, Berkshire and Wiltshire Regiment (RGBW), now amalgamated into The Rifles. I recall a song playing in the background that I really liked at the time and I still play to this day called *My United States of Whatever* by Liam Lynch. I also remember feeling generally relaxed and at ease while talking to the sergeant, enjoying a feeling of being at home within the military whose sense of humour is different from that in civilian life, much of it based on banter between comrades.

I had two or three meetings with the sergeant over a period of time, discussing where I would go, which part of the armed forces I would join and where I would undergo my training. There were a number of choices open to me regarding training; although approaching the age of seventeen, I would still be joining the Army as what is known as a 'boy soldier.' I had to choose between the standard twenty-four weeks training at the Infantry Training Centre at Catterick, in North Yorkshire, or a longer period of training at the Army Foundation College at Harrogate. Despite the fact that those who were trained at Harrogate tended to be promoted a little more rapidly, I decided that I wanted to complete my training as soon as possible and so opted for Catterick.

My first day in the British Army for training was Valentine's Day 2003, but not exactly filled with romance! I made my way down to the Army Training Regiment at Pirbright to undergo the selection process for the Army, which lasted two days. Having previously trained hard to pass the three-day selection assessment for the Royal Marines, which I had come so very close to achieving, I experienced little difficulty with the Army tests because of my high level of physical fitness

One of these was the 'bleep test' where you have to run a certain distance before the bleep sounds and back again before it sounds again and so on, until too exhausted to make it before the next bleep. There was a target of fourteen bleeps set by the Royal Marines and twelve for the Army. I completed sixteen and can recall, as everyone dropped out, myself and another lad sprinting back and forwards like mad men for what seemed an eternity. We also underwent a number of command tasks. I remember one in particular where there were mats, vaulting horses and other items of gymnasium equipment neatly arranged to resemble cannons. We had to work in teams of four or five, dismantling our cannon and carrying it from one mat before reassembling it. I was placed in charge of my team and generally tried to do what I thought was correct, such as taking command, making decisions and issuing orders.

Other tests included completing a timed mile and a half run. In the Royal Marines it was three miles, so once again my previous training paid off and I completed the test without any difficulty. Those two days at Pirbright cemented my enjoyment of Army life. I had been used to living away from home, spending time with my father in Reading and my mother in Peterborough, so homesickness was not a problem for me. That, together with my high level of physical fitness, made things easier and not too daunting. I was, of course, somewhat naïve. I remember thinking that I would join the Army and be allowed to choose the job I wanted, in my case to be a member of a sniper platoon. This is most definitely not the case, because selection for the platoon is based on skills and aptitude for the role.

For the moment, anyway, I had passed the selection tests for the Army and now had to undergo training as an infantryman. If, in due course, I wanted to become a sniper I would have to win my place in platoon on merit alone.

CHAPTER 2

Training at Catterick

On arrival at the Infantry Training Centre at Catterick, I found a real mix of characters of whom the majority were from the north of England with only around four or five of us coming from southern counties. I was initially nicknamed the 'posh sounding bloke' or on occasions something less polite. As we got to know each other during the first few weeks, I became more widely known as, 'Soap Dish' because I used to put my cigarettes in a soap dish to stop them getting crushed or wet in the rain. I suppose everyone has to be called something. I thought it was a brilliant idea, but it did not catch on and everyone else thought it was funny.

Training did not prove to be particularly tough for me, nothing like that shown in films such as *Full Metal Jacket*, for example, which depicted basic training in the 1960s US Marine style. I do remember that it was initially a bit of a shock to the system sharing a room with three or four other guys for the first time in my life. This strange experience was further compounded by the fact that for the first six weeks we were not allowed to have any luxuries at all. We were not permitted to go home or allowed to wear berets at this stage, wearing what were known as 'crow caps': peaked combat caps which signify the newest batch of recruits who know nothing.

At this early stage of our training the only proper contact we had was with each other. I do remember our section commander literally ordering us to write a letter home. His name was Corporal Hindmarsh, a proper Geordie who was really quite an amusing guy and who, fortunately for me, took a shine to me. He really knew his stuff, was fair and did not muck any of us about. We liked and respected him for his knowledge and skills although, to be fair, all of the corporals really knew their stuff as the army tended to pick the best of the bunch from the infantry to be instructors at Catterick. The standard of training was high and after completing a two-year posting at the Infantry Training Centre, instructors were either promoted, if already qualified for the next rank up, or sent on a promotion course.

After the initial six weeks training, things became a little easier and we were allowed to have just a few of life's luxuries that had been lacking up until that point. These were just simple things that you would normally take for granted in normal life – televisions, DVD players and being permitted to put up posters. This extended to being allowed to have duvets, whereas previously we had to make our beds in the old school way with sheets, blankets and 'hospital corners.' The latter, along with literally every aspect of our kit, were inspected almost daily and I lost count of the number of times my bed was torn apart. In fact, it became such a frequent occurrence that I decided to save time in the morning before an inspection by making my bed perfectly the night before and sleeping on the floor in my sleeping bag. At one point we were actually shown how to shave; looking back on it now, I suppose we were all still very young at that time and I think I had only actually shaved twice in my life up to that point.

Our training was conducted stage by stage, and we carried out day and a half long exercises with rifles that contained no ammunition, so we could simply get used to the feel of them while performing these tasks in full equipment. We then progressed to three-day exercises and then ones lasting up to a week, which I think was the longest at Catterick. I enjoyed the bayonet training which lasted all day, two days being devoted to this in all. I remember it particularly because it was different in the sense that it was adrenalin fuelled training all through the day. We were normally woken up at 5.00 am each morning; on this particular morning we were woken at 4.00 am. This was not a gentle ruffle of the hair and an, 'OK sunshine, time to wake up.' On the contrary, it was like a bomb going off in the room. The lights were snapped on and the instructors came in banging things, kicking the bins, punching the doors, throwing the duvets off us and literally dragging us out of bed without warning. I remember all of us leaping out of our beds as the room echoed to shouts of, 'Stand by your beds! Stand by your beds!', feeling dazed and not quite with it. Corporal Hindmarsh shouted that we had five seconds to tear apart each other's lockers.

We really did not want to do that because we all knew just how long it took to making our bedspaces perfect. But we did, following which we were dragged out in to the freezing corridor in our boxer shorts, not permitted to say anything or look at anyone. All the while we were subjected to a constant stream of verbal abuse, being accused of not taking care of our kits and bedspace areas. There were taunts of, 'You're nothing! You want to be soldiers? You'll never be soldiers!' After that we were sent off to get dressed but not to look at or speak to anyone. Woe betide anyone who was caught even making eye contact, let alone talking to anyone, the punishment being made to do countless press-ups and similar exercises to the point of exhaustion.

We were then marched down to the armoury where the instructors drilled us with shouts of, 'what's a bayonet for?' and, 'what's it made of?.' In return, we would respond with shouts of, 'cold hard steel!.' The instructors were winding us up as much as possible. They were successful, and I for one understood the aim of the exercise.

We were running across a football pitch, falling to the ground when a whistle blew and then jumping to our feet when the whistle blew again. It was pouring with rain and the ground was waterlogged, so we were covered in mud and soaked through. It was also very slippery, and running around carrying rifles with fixed bayonets in such conditions was deemed too dangerous; consequently, due to health and safety regulations, we could only run without our weapons. Eventually, utterly exhausted, covered in mud and soaked, we were marched through to a field where the instructors had erected a number of dummies with red paint balloons inside them. We were ordered initially to walk up to the dummies screaming our heads off, ensuring we stabbed them a couple of times. If anyone did not attack the dummies with sufficient aggression or scream vigorously enough, the whole platoon was ordered to run to the farthest tree on the training field and back in the driving rain. While we did this, cursing the man in question but laughing all the same, we had to drop to the floor as the whistle was blown and then jump up again. This went on for a further four or five hours. To finish off the day, the dummies were laid out in a circuit and we were required to crawl along with our rifles, stabbing like mad men each time we reached a prone dummy. When we reached the last dummy, we unfixed the bayonet from the rifle and used it as a knife to stab the dummy.

We finally finished and were marched back to the barracks for something to eat, being allowed to talk again and treated as being human again. Bizarre though this may seem and despite how it sounds, at the age of seventeen it was actually one of the most fun things I had ever done and I really enjoyed it. I must admit to looking back at that day often and, in hindsight with an adult perspective, often chuckle while remembering how at that time I was having the time of my life and loving every minute of it.

At the end of twelve weeks of training, Corporal Hindmarsh left us to do the senior Brecon course to qualify him for promotion to sergeant, before rejoining his battalion of the Royal Regiment of Fusiliers because his two-year stint as an instructor at the ITC had come to an end. He was replaced by another Geordie called Corporal Norris, who also proved to be a good guy. At this point I was transferred to another section commanded by a mad Irishman called Corporal Cree whom I also liked and, more importantly, respected. Subsequently, I was transferred yet again to another section because of various injuries that occurred and was required to go through the process of, 'back squadding' for failure to make the grade. My last section commander wore the same cap badge as me, that of the Royal Anglian Regiment, but seemed to be prejudiced against those due to go to the 1st Battalion (known as The Vikings) rather than his own unit, the 2nd Battalion (The Poachers). This was disappointing, but I put it down to being all part of the real world and politics.

Our training continued on through all its stages, including the

Annual Personal Weapons Test, which we had to pass, and on through more skill at arms training with assessment, including shooting up to 400 metres with our SA80 A1 rifles. I achieved marksman level on this assessment and was awarded the prize for best shot in my platoon, which was a sign of things to come. I still have that little tankard with my name engraved on it to this day. In fact, I always have a pint out of it on Christmas Day as my own little tradition as another member of the family that has been awarded for his marksmanship. It always makes me smile.

Eventually, at the end of twenty-four weeks, I completed my training and on 26 September 2003 I passed out of ITC Catterick with the family there for our passing-out parade. I remember the day as being really nice and sunny, which was a fitting end to an enjoyable period and a great start to my first two weeks leave.

On 6 October 2003, at not quite eighteen years of age, I joined the 1st Battalion The Royal Anglian Regiment and was posted to No. 9 Platoon, of C Company, which was for me at the time absolutely living the dream.

CHAPTER 3

Becoming a Viking

On arriving at Elizabeth Barracks in Pirbright, Surrey, I recognised the roads from my previous time there. It is a large camp and although I still felt comfortable and at ease, the two suicides at the nearby Deepcut Barracks, which were much in the news at the time and still being investigated, came to mind. I did not really know what to expect of life in the battalion, having heard rumours and people telling me that the first six months is totally bad until you earn your right to be there. There were tales of the training we had just completed being an utter doddle and that in the battalion you would be literally punched in the face if you make a mistake – that is the real Army, so be prepared. I did not dwell on this too much and decided to approach things with an open mind. I have to admit that I was unable to quell my anxiety completely but such feelings are normal in any walk of life, on the first day in school or starting a new job.

As I approached the front gate, what I did not realise at the time was that the guys on duty were actually from my platoon in C Company. I appeared laden with four huge kit bags, containing literally everything, including all of my clothing, boots and helmet, and looking like some military answer to Steptoe and Son. I had decided not to use the internal army postal system, which was notorious for its inconsistency.

On arriving I arrived in front of my new comrades, and being used to the drill at Catterick, I stamped to a halt as if I were on a parade square, shouting my army number and announcing that Private Cartwright was, 'Reporting for duty, Sir.' The reaction from the lance corporal and his soldiers was rapturous applause and cheering to which I responded by also laughing. At that moment I thought, 'Yes, I will be right at home here.' It is that kind of squaddy mentality that I loved and still do. Inwardly I was calling myself an idiot, but I guess I just didn't know what to expect and could only put it down to experience.

A guy called Freddy showed me up to meet the Company Sergeant Major and others, and eventually I was introduced to a very short and skinny lance corporal named Simon Pimm who came across saying, 'Oh, you're the new bloke then.' He offered to take me up to the barracks, to which I replied, 'Yes Corporal', as this was exactly how we had been taught at Catterick to behave, showing proper respect.

This somewhat stinted conversation continued as we made our way towards the barracks, with me replying, 'Yes Corporal' to everything he said. Finally he stopped, turned to me and said quietly, 'Listen mate, if you call me Corporal one more time, I'm going to punch you in the face.' I replied, 'Oh sorry,' before he simply told me to call him Bog Rat like everyone else did.

I still laugh about my first moments there. It was quite a shock because throughout all my brief Army career up to that point, it had been drilled into me that I must call everyone this and that and ensure that I stood to attention. Everyone had to be called by their rank, unless it was an officer or warrant officer, in which case it would be, 'Sir.' Anyway, Bog Rat told me about the people I would be with, who had recently returned from a tour of Northern Ireland and were really quite cliquey, warning me not to expect to fit in and make friends too quickly which, to be honest, filled me with dread. I had visions of them being war hardened and having had a really rough time; in truth, they had actually had quite an easy time with nothing having occurred at all.

There was one guy, Ben Emmett, whom I had known during training who was put into my room. That made things a little easier, but by and large the guys from 9 Platoon were all pretty cool. I soon made friends with a number of them and was given as a mentor, someone with the nickname, 'Billy Whiz.' He was a really good lad and was also friendly with another guy called, 'Webby' who was the platoon clown, having a reputation as someone who would always be on the piss and a really good laugh. It was decided that Billy Whiz would be my, 'in barracks' mentor while Webby would be my, 'on the piss' mentor.

As my second mentor, Webby came into his own after a few weeks when a company party was organised and I became so mortally drunk it was almost the talk of the barracks. A load of Skol lager, had been brought by some of the lads which hardly anyone wanted to drink, but Webby of course encouraged me to do so. I think everyone had taken a few cans but, apart from the fact that the lager was largely ignored, not being the company's desired booze of choice. Annoyed by the lack of people drinking their generous contribution, the lads announced that the bar would not be opening until every last can of Skol had been downed. Needless to say, I being the new guy had been passed literally everyone else's cans. Nowadays, a large quantity of Skol would not be on my Christmas list but at the time this seemed like a particularly cheap night. I didn't care that it was Skol, merely that it was free and alcoholic. There were around fifteen or twenty cans left and I put almost all of them away. This made me blind drunk, and I mean properly drunk, to the point that Billy Whiz literally had to hold me up as he took me back to my room at around 1.00 or 2.00 am in the morning, before presenting me with a sick bucket and disappearing.

Before long us new arrivals in the battalion were taken off to the ranges to zero our rifles. There were four of us: Ben Emmett, Ike Smith, Nicky Waite and me. During our training at Catterick we had used the SA80 A1 rifle but were now given the new SA80 A2, which was a very much better weapon. I can still remember receiving mine still covered in the grease in which it had left the factory. There was not one scratch on it and it was literally out of the wrapper and brand spanking new. I was the first person ever to fire this weapon and I appreciated it. I remember thinking how beautiful it was to shoot, being so accurate. I felt guilty even making it slightly dirty.

It didn't take long before I managed to demonstrate my shooting ability against individuals who had been in the battalion for three or four years and even some of the NCOs. I managed to beat their scores by simply producing better grouping. I think at that point I was achieving a group of approximately 30mm. A bullet from an SA80 is 5.56mm in diameter and so to achieve that kind of score I needed to put five rounds into a 3.0cm group from a range of 100 metres, which took some achievement.

At the end of the day on the range I was walking back to the transport and Sergeant Neil shouted across, 'Come on then, Cartwright. Get into that truck over there on the left.' I walked across to the vehicle whose large canvas canopy flap at the rear was down. I lifted this to one side, to be confronted by soldiers all staring down at me with cigarette smoke billowing out around them. At that point one of them shouted out, 'Ere, does your mum know you're here?' Of course everyone fell about laughing as I was a new guy with the particularly baby face I possessed at that time. Everyone was laughing as I jumped aboard muttering, 'Ha ha, very funny,' with a big grin on my face. The thought that I had got lost on the way to the chip shop, having been sent by my mother and wandered into the Recruitment Office, induced a grudging, 'Nice one, guys' from me as they all fell about laughing.

Despite the relative success of my first shooting experience, it took time to be noticed and it was some seven or eight months before I made my first attempt to be selected for the Sniper Platoon.

The first proper exercise in which I took part was on Salisbury Plain during the first two weeks of December 2003, when the weather was absolutely freezing. I really cannot describe how cold that was. We lived in Copehill Down, which was the FIBUA (Fighting In Built-Up Areas) village and we always referred to it as the FISH Village, which stood for, 'Fighting In Someone's House.' It was where we practised storming houses, jumping through windows, throwing grenades through doorways and generally learning the skills of FIBUA. We lived in this village, which sadly had no glass in the windows and no heating and was utterly freezing.

For the initial period we were out for a day and then for two days as a run-up to the full exercise. My section commander at the time was a guy called Corporal Gary Stewart who was actually quite a decent bloke and a horse of a man. His second-in-command was Lance

BECOMING A VIKING

Corporal Kev Langston who really was a good laugh and could do a
thing called the wind surfer which was the ability to transform his nut
sack (testicle bag) by almost impossible means, into the shape of a
wind surfer which became the stuff of legend. I think there maybe a
photo of this somewhere, alongside other miracles like an invention
called, 'the cheeseburger' which really does amazingly resemble a
cheeseburger and strangely uses all of his genitalia. I know it sounds
totally juvenile but, when you are within this environment, this really
was the kind of silly thing that was really funny and made Army life
fun.

I remember the last phase of the final and main exercise was an
attack on the village of Imber. The Commanding Officer had got
himself into a bit of a flap and we were marched at really high pace
into the valley, despite carrying heavy packs and full kit, and
consequently arrived around two hours early at 1.00 am, pouring with
sweat, but the attack was not scheduled to being until 3.00 am. We lay
up in a valley, watching the minutes going by. My combat jacket and
t-shirt were literally drenched with sweat and before long the icy wind
and freezing temperature, heralded by a mist that rolled into the valley
and formed a heavy frost, began to take effect. Having lost so much
fluid through sweat, I was gulping water from my water bottle.
Eventually we received the order to prepare to move. While readying
myself and organising my kit properly, I checked my pockets and the
various zip fasteners on my clothing. As I did so, I discovered that,
while drinking, I had dribbled on to a couple of zips which had literally
frozen solid with ice. You can imagine how we felt, lying there
motionless and freezing.

After about an hour to an hour and a half, we were ordered to our
feet and marched out and then back into the valley. This was done in
an attempt to warm us up because by then three or four of our number
had been taken away suffering from hypothermia and the early
warning signs of frostbite.

As we marched back in again, we commenced the attack. My
section's role was to provide flanking support for another section as it
entered one of the main buildings. However we were subjected to a

13

major counter-attack that resulted in everyone in my section being killed apart from me, due to my being positioned on the other side of a large shrub. This was more to do with my becoming separated from my group in the darkness and confusion; to be honest, I probably was not concentrating as much as I should have been because of the freezing conditions. Each of us was equipped with the Personal Role Radio (PRR) and I made contact with the second-in-command of the section, Kev, and asked what was happening. His response was to order me to sneak along the main track towards the main body of the enemy in the area; I should initially throw a grenade and then open fire with my rifle. Preparing a grenade and switching my SA80 to automatic fire mode, I sneaked along the track until I heard voices, thereafter creeping forward and adopting the best possible position. Readying myself, I threw the grenade and, as soon as it exploded, charged out with rifle blazing.

Unfortunately, and I still laugh about it now, I tripped over a root and fell hard and ungracefully on my face. Everyone, of course, fell about with laughter while mocking taunts of, 'Nice one Rambo, you only killed three people,' rang in my ears. I did of course protest, saying that, despite my tripping up , I had fired a number of rounds and thrown a grenade that had exploded in the middle of the main group. Despite my embarrassment, I maintained I had killed more than three of them.

Filling the air with banter, we all extracted our cookers from our packs and organised a fire to huddle around in an effort to keep warm. Eventually dawn arrived, bringing with it the sun. Endex (end of exercise) was called and with great relief we headed for our Saxon armoured personnel carriers for the return journey to Westdown Camp.

Each Saxon was equipped with fire extinguishers. Normally, they were activated by pulling a safety pin and then pressing a button. This particular type could be set off by banging the top of it which resulted in a non-stop massive flow of frothy foam. On this occasion, one of B Company's Saxons had driven in and hit a massive pothole, the impact setting off an extinguisher inside the vehicle. The result was hilarious; when the door opened, a number of snowmen staggered out covered in foam from top to toe. We all just split our sides laughing! It was perfect timing for this to happen when everyone was so relieved to be going home after such a long and cold exercise. B Company covered in white foam – priceless! I don't think I will ever forget that moment. Learning a lot, making lifelong friends and forming lifelong memories, that one so funny, were some of the best aspects of my early days in the battalion.

9 Platoon, although we were always proud of it, was always undermanned and this discriminated against us during competitions because we tended to lose, sometimes by quite some margin. There were only sixteen of us, whereas a full-strength platoon numbered thirty-two men in three sections of eight men and a platoon headquarters, so we were at half-strength while the other two platoons in our company, 10 and 11 Platoons, were well up to strength.

Meanwhile, I remained very keen to join the Sniper Platoon. I had discovered from a guy who had previously completed the sniper course that you had to have served for at least six months before you could even be selected or put forward for the course. Eventually, due to the time I had served and possessing a certain degree of aptitude, I was allowed to attempt selection for the snipers. The platoon had only two vacancies for which there were twelve candidates. This was soon whittled down to seven and eventually, following a few injuries, there were only five of us left. One of these was a guy called Alex Hawkins who passed on this attempt. This was the first time I had met him and we got on really well. I would come into contact with him again in due course, but for now our paths parted as I unfortunately failed on this attempt to join the platoon. However this was the summer of 2004 and the beginning of an exciting period in my army career, beginning with a move to the Brigade Surveillance Company for a forthcoming tour of operations tour in Iraq.

CHAPTER 4

Becoming a Sniper

On returning from Iraq, I was still utterly determined to try again for sniper selection. This time I was successful, being one of twelve who passed out of the seventeen candidates who attempted selection.

I was so proud to have been accepted into the Sniper Platoon although I never became what is known as a 'badged' sniper, something that was always a source of great disappointment to me. I was so very close, but on the Badge Tests I just always seemed to be a few points short. There was always a huge degree of pride and achievement attached to being 'badged' and to some of the older members of the platoon, you were considered an incredibly good 'sharpshooter' rather than a sniper. Despite this, I was now a member of the platoon, doing exactly the same as everyone else. It was probably more just me, but I felt that maybe I lacked the same level achievement as the 'badged' guys. That said, as time went on and with us doing exactly the job, my attitude was that, sharpshooter or sniper, I was still in the platoon, wearing a ghillie suit and carrying an L96A1 sniper rifle – I had passed selection and felt I could consider myself pretty damned good because of it.

I remember the first day I met Alex again, along with Teddy. We were in a four-man room together. Apart from some periodical changes of personnel, we all found life in the platoon relatively easy. Deano, Cas, and Kingy had passed selection as well and came from C Company. CD and Burney came from A Company. TM and Teddy both came from B Company. Jock and OB both came from HQ

Company and LC joined from the Brigade Surveillance Company. Two other members were Robbo and Spud had been in the platoon for years, both being 'badged.'

We would go down for muster parade at around 8.00 am in the morning and then head off for our platoon training. One subject, for example, was observation training. We would be given an hour to sketch a panoramic view of what we could observe. We would need to enter detail facing north, south, east or west, marking in the left and right of arc of fire and our location. We would observe and note key ranges where there might be a prominent road or a fallen tree. In addition, we had to locate certain items of military equipment pre-positioned in the area under observation for us to spot, such as a bayonet stuck in the ground, a radio antenna poking up from amongst reeds or a bush, or other items such as rifle magazines, radio batteries or a flare launcher. Using binoculars and telescopes, we would have to search for and log anything we saw, being awarded points for items observed, measuring bearings correctly, plotting arcs of fire and logging other information. Attention to detail was always paramount in the Sniper Platoon.

I would have liked to have spent more time on the ranges but, when you consider that we used almost a year's allocation of 7.62mm sniper grade ammunition during a single badge test, it is probably understandable why this was not possible. We shot at ranges of up to 900 metres and were awarded ten points for a hit on a target at 900 metres from a cold barrel. Out of all the times I attempted this, which was only perhaps eight occasions, I succeeded six times. We learned to shoot in all weather conditions; one of the few times I failed to hit the target was in pouring rain with a very high wind.

I remember that we all wanted to practise shooting from helicopters, but our NCO instructors just laughed, because that was not going to happen. Life in the Sniper Platoon was different to that in the rest of the battalion, as was the mentality of the NCOs who treated us with a lot more respect. I noticed other subtle changes too, such as the way the guys from the rifle companies looked up to us. They would not admit it of course, but one could tell, particularly on those occasions when the whole battalion was assembled and the Sniper Platoon was formed up together. This was probably because we were one of the elements in the battalion that you had to be selected for, which made it all just a little different and somehow special. I really loved being part of it.

I had just turned twenty years of age and was really quite happy with life because I had done a tour of Iraq, had succeeded in joining the snipers on merit and was where I wanted to be. Looking back, I do not think I would have been able to imagine life becoming much better until I was put forward to be selected for promotion to lance corporal, which was what eventually happened. Out of around sixty people who went for promotion, only thirty-two passed and I came ninth. I was one of the more junior on the list, so this was quite an achievement for me. Unfortunately, the Commanding Officer was only selecting the top eight candidates for promotion on that particular occasion. I did not have to wait long because only three months later I was promoted.

CHAPTER 5

Life as a Sniper

On joining the Sniper Platoon, I was put into Robbo's section, which was equipped with what became my nightmare: quad bikes. We were given some training on them and received what would normally be called a licence, but we called it a conversion. We were out on exercise with them all the time, doing really steep hill climbs and hill descents sometimes with a trailer sometimes not, but generally becoming proficient on them by day and night, navigating and moving from point to point. I was the first to roll my quad and this became a pattern for me that continued. Whereas the other guys took to the quads like ducks to water, I struggled and really did not like them. To begin with I thought they were fun but, as we went off on exercise over terrain that had been churned up by tanks and then set like rock in the sun, the going became really difficult. I cannot recall the number of times I fell off my machine, to the point that it became really frustrating and not fun at all. I just could not seem to get to grips with it.

Tom, on the other hand, turned out to be a 'Quad God' because he had been riding them since he was around eight years old, while Robbo and LC were both guys who were just good at everything they did. But then there was me. On our first exercise with the quads, we were on Salisbury plain following the Reconnaissance Platoon in its Scimitar CVR-Ts (Combat Vehicle Reconnaissance Tracked – a type of light tank). We had pushed forward miles ahead of the rifle platoons and were clearing woods and locating enemy positions. Robbo and I had split up from LC and Tom and we were just behind a CVR-T when its commander told us that he needed to cross some open ground but was unhappy that a wood in the distance to the west had not been cleared. He asked Robbo if we could dart across and clear it for him.

We made our way towards the wood, using the low ground for cover. Rounding a corner, we came across a huge puddle with very high banks. Robbo began to traverse across the edge while I gave him cover. As he got half way across his quad rolled into the water, pinning him underwater. Dropping my rifle and jumping off my quad, I dashed to help him. His head surfaced as he shouted, 'JC! JC!' before slipping back underwater. I yelled, 'I'm coming! I'm coming!' as I ran splashing into the muddy water which was waist deep. Groping below the water, I grabbed the quad and heaved with a huge grunt like an Olympic weightlifter. I felt Robbo's hands grab my ankles before he swam between my legs and surfaced behind me gasping for breath.

Later that day, Robbo opened his ammunition container which held, among other things, all his food and took out a packet of tortillas which he was going to use for a sandwich. The packet was already opened, and the soaked tortillas were just like chamois leathers. Just as I lit a cigarette, he threw one at me and it hit me square on the face, slapping and wrapping around it like a face hugger from the film *Aliens*. Such was life with us, and it was good stuff.

Such was my dislike of the quads that eventually I asked if I could move to another section. Shortly afterwards, the announcement came that we were going to Afghanistan for deployment into Helmand province, so everything changed. Bernie was terminating and so was posted to help train Lithuanian snipers. LC also terminated at the same time as Spud, and right at the last moment we took on another four guys: Vinny, Jimmy, Scotty and Dan. So, with Deano, Tom, Alex and me now being promoted, we were appointed as section commanders and seconds-in-command (2IC). No. 1 Section had Jock in command with CD (Donnie) as 2IC, with OB and Jimmy as shooters. They were to be attached to A Company. No. 2 Section had Deano in command with myself as 2IC with Teddy and Scotty as the shooters, and was to be attached to B Company. Teddy was my shooter – the more experienced shooter went with the 2IC while the other was paired with the section commander. No. 3 Section had Robbo in command with Tom as 2IC and Cas and Dan as shooters. They were to be attached to C Company. No. 4 Section was commanded by Mo (an old school sniper) with Alex as 2IC and Kingy and Vinny as shooters.

At this time, we changed from the manoeuvre support groups (MSG) role to that of fire support groups (FSG), which also incorporated the Machine Gun and Anti-Tank Platoons, this being a lesson learned from 3 PARA which was the first battalion to deploy into Helmand the year before. Unlike us, the Paras had to construct their forward bases, which they called Platoon Houses, whilst under attack from the enemy; at the same time, they were tasked with driving the enemy back through offensive action. This was really hard tough work.

We were equipped for our new role with the new L115A1 .338 sniper rifle. A formidable weapon, it was bigger, heavier and louder than the L96A1 sniper rifles we had used previously in the UK. The L96A1 is a very accurate and powerful rifle but on operations in Helmand we mainly used the L115A1 which, being a larger calibre weapon and firing a more powerful round, performed better at longer ranges.

The snipers were generally pretty popular, particularly among the officers who seemed to think we were the best thing since sliced bread. The platoon sergeants also thought we were pretty cool. We knew these guys quite well because at this point I had served with the Royal Anglians for four years and there were actually a few sergeants in B Company who were corporals in C Company when I was there. Joel Adlington was a full corporal in B Company and I had known him since we were both privates in C Company. Jay, later promoted to Sergeant, used to be a sniper and was now a section commander in B Company. I knew him quite well as he had trained us on our sniper cadre. Equally, there were quite a few new guys whom I did not know who were really good lads and a brilliant laugh. All in all, my section was filled with a great bunch of excellent soldiers who were a great laugh and we all got on well.

Although our forthcoming deployment would be for six months, in reality a tour of operations lasts for a year because the six months beforehand are devoted to training under the supervision of the Operational Training Advisory Group (OPTAG). The training programme consists of exercise after exercise with the battalion away a lot of the time and constantly undergoing more and more fitness for role training at the same time.

One example of this took place every Friday when, before we could go home, we had to do what is referred to as the 'CO's Blow.' As the name suggests, this is a real fitness blow-out and the Commanding Officer selects what the battalion does for fitness. Approaching final deployment, it reached to the point where we were doing almost decathlons in full kit weighing around 50 pounds. As part of the FSG the snipers, along with the Machine Gun and Anti-Tank Platoons, were made to run miles with full kit while also carrying jerrycans full of water. This was exhausting and unfortunately only one part of the 'CO's Blow' as we would then have to push Land Rovers up an upward sloping road, then run around to do a full assault course followed by a three-mile steeplechase run before carrying the biggest fattest bloke from the MT (motor transport) Platoon all the way back to barracks. We would then have to carry large tyres and heavy chains along with other things around for two or three hours. All this training was essential because it would undoubtedly give us the edge on the enemy during operations.

As part of our pre-deployment training, we also spent five weeks on exercise in Kenya, the aim of which was firstly to ensure that we became acclimatised to extreme heat but also to prepare us for forthcoming operations. This began with section tactics, progressing through platoon to company attacks. The companies underwent the training programme individually in the same order they would be deployed to Afghanistan, which was A, C and B.

CHAPTER 6

Deployment

An infantry battalion comprises three rifle companies, a support company, and a headquarter Company. Each rifle company consists of three platoons, with a platoon comprising three sections and a platoon headquarters. Each company has its own headquarters element consisting of the officer commanding (OC), the second-in-command (2IC,) the company sergeant major (CSM), the company quartermaster sergeant (CQMS) and his storemen who are responsible for the organisation and issue of the company's stores, rations, ammunition and equipment.

I was in D Company, which comprised the sniper, reconnaissance, mortar, machine gun and anti-tank platoons. The latter were always referred to as the Javelin Platoon, that being the name of missile system with which it was equipped. The Javelin is a fire-and-forget system; locking on to the target whilst still in its launching tube and then tracking it during flight right up to the moment of impact and detonation It is a really good bit of kit, albeit each missile costs £40,000. During the coming months our battle group would fire 142 of these missiles during operations in Afghanistan. You don't need a calculator to work out that particular of the cost of war. We were shown film footage of a Javelin destroying an old tank to give us an idea of the destructive power of the weapon. On watching it Caz said, 'I don't quite know what I was expecting, maybe the Monty Python foot to come down or something.'

The fire support groups (FSG) that made up D Company were attached to A, B and C companies, with my own supporting B

Company. We spent a few weeks packing all of our kit and handing in our MFO boxes with 'comfy kit' which would be transported by sea to Afghanistan. Meanwhile we took two weeks pre-deployment leave.

I saw a lot of my family during this leave. We all knew I was going into a real war zone and that inevitably there would be casualties. I remember my brother saying, 'Don't be a hero. Just do your job, nothing more and nothing less.' Having to say goodbye to my girlfriend Annie was very hard and although we had been apart before, through the Iraq tour and exercises elsewhere, we both knew that this would be very different. I had come across a video on YouTube that the Paras had made during their tour of Afghanistan a year previously and I was well aware that it gave an accurate picture. I watched it over and over again in an attempt to familiarise myself with the type of terrain and the likely tasks we would be performing. Annie watched it with me and was not happy at all and, after watching the dangers I would face, she became more and more apprehensive about me going. In fairness, she never moaned or asked me to quit because she knew it was what I wanted to do. She was really very good about it, although it was clearly hard at times for her, supporting me all the way, which was fantastic. This demonstrated to me the strength of the bond between us, and the depth of her love for me.

As we said our goodbyes, my father told me how proud he was of me and I remember mentioning that he could now probably understand how his father must have felt when he himself went off to the Falklands War. I felt there was a close bond between us just then, which others were unable to share, because of the unique circumstances my father and I shared. Everyone put on a brave face and continued telling me how proud they were of me. Now, I just wanted to go and get the job done and come home in one piece. I had no idea then just how many times I would come close to being killed.

Following a long and emotional goodbye to everyone, my mother drove me back to the barracks. I can recall the car journey being pretty quiet for the most part. I was suffering from the same sort of nerves or butterflies that you experienced at school when the bell had just rung for lunch break and you were on the way to the playground where a bully was waiting to punch you.

When we finally arrived at the barracks, I remember it being really quite a sunny and warm day and the area seemed almost deserted. All the other companies were already deployed in Afghanistan, and it was strange to see the place so quiet. We both walked through to my room, which I shared with Dan and Alex. My kit was all ready on the bed, so I did my final checks making sure all my magazines were there and that I had emptied my water bottles to ensure that there was no water in them to become stagnant by the time I arrived. Going down sick on one's first day on operations would not have gone down very well at all.

I could see the tears welling up in my mother's eyes as we stood by the car, saying goodbye. She held on to me as if she was resisting letting go, promising to write to me and send parcels. It was surreal feeling and, in the back of my mind, there was the thought that this could be the very last time I would see my mother. I remember trying to brush it all off by saying that everything would be fine, that there were no problems at all, and telling her to keep her chin up and stop being silly.

After my mother had gone, Deano and Scotty arrived and I quickly changed into uniform ready for the first parade. Off we then went for muster parade, dressed in our fresh, clean, perfectly pressed desert combat clothing with the badges all in the right places. Soon we were all catching up on what we had got up to during our leave. It was normal stuff, but amongst this slightly high spirited chatter we were also talking about things we had seen online about Afghanistan, similar to the video I had seen on YouTube, and saying how mad it all looked. It was a scene of mixed feelings once again.

After the parade, we went back to our rooms to chill out while we waited to leave. Later, as we went to the cookhouse for our evening meal, the trucks and coaches began to arrive. My kit weighed an absolute ton and dug in to my shoulders, but we needed to carry things for every eventuality, including being delayed and having to stay overnight somewhere en route. We all piled on to the transport and I remember it being dark by the time we left. I tried to get some sleep as we drove towards our first destination, South Cerney, where we were checked-in and handed in our bags. We were held there for around four or five hours which seemed like an eternity.

As a soldier, I always considered myself fortunate having the surname Cartwright because in the Army everything is always done in alphabetical order and so I was always one of the first to be called. As I walked around the departures area before we left for RAF Brize Norton, I noticed that people were tending to group with their closest friends. This was probably even more the case with those of us in the FSG because we were split up among the rifle companies. In some instances, this would continue throughout the whole forthcoming tour, even though many new friendships would be forged.

We finally arrived at RAF Brize Norton where we all sat around in our groups, waiting for the off. The aircraft arrived in the form of an RAF Tri-Star which took us on an eight-hour flight to Kandahar, which was one of the provinces adjoining Helmand Province in the south of Afghanistan. We were served normal airline type food, but there were no in-flight movies. During the flight, I sat next to a member of B Company whom we had got to know during the six months of training.

During that time, most of our instructors were Paras whom we had watched on YouTube. They had handed over to 42 Commando RM whom we were relieving. Despite my having failed to join the Royal Marines, I was still going to end up fighting in Helmand and so it somehow seemed like destiny. That led me to thinking perhaps I would not come back, that perhaps I would die out there. Eventually, I came to the conclusion that there was nothing I could do to control my fate, no matter how fast I ran or how low I crawled. If I was going to be wounded or killed, then it would happen.

As we approached Kandahar, I checked my kit because we needed to keep our body armour and helmets with us at all times. Although it is not mentioned on the news, Kandahar airport is attacked regularly. At that time, there were still Taliban operating in Kandahar and the Canadians were responsible for the area. The British did not see much actual fighting in Kandahar as the majority of their troops were based in Helmand. When you consider that Afghanistan is around four or five times the size of the United Kingdom and Helmand is the size of Wales, that puts it into perspective – it is a big place.

We landed at the huge air base under cover of darkness, because landings only take place at night to avoid aircraft becoming targets of ground fire. On arrival, we moved into what can only be described as one massive air conditioned tent. As I came down the stairs of the plane the overriding feeling was that, 'There are thousands of people here that want to kill me.' The other thing that hit me was the sheer intensity of the heat. It was so incredibly humid, similar to when you step off an air conditioned aircraft when going on holiday. The big difference was that there was no suntan lotion and cold beer waiting for us.

We climbed aboard buses which took us to a massive sand-coloured air conditioned tent that looked like a huge hollowed out bouncy castle in which you could fit two or three tennis courts. There we found massive fridge freezers with ice cold bottled water displaying large signs saying, 'Cold bottle out – hot bottle in.' There were strict rules on smoking, with huge bins provided for cigarette butts of which there were only three. Large quantities were scattered around the bins – typical squaddies, nothing changes.

We arrived in time for the evening meal, along with coachloads of other troops coming from the flight line into the main camp. The sheer size of the base was almost overwhelming, its facilities a whole world apart from those at British bases. We drove past floodlit American football pitches and tennis courts, as well as Burger King, Pizza Hut and Subway fast food outlets. You could buy embroidered t-shirts, Persian rugs, perfume, alcohol-free beer and all manner of things ranging from Play Station 3s through to beef jerky. All of us wanted to head for the American cookhouse as it was reputedly so much better than its British equivalent, with everything you could want. Unfortunately, it was closing as it was late so we ended up eating British food.

Having eaten, we were shown to our sleeping quarters for the night. Once again, these were massive: an area the size of two football pitches with bunk beds almost as far as the eye could see. We all crashed out for the night. I had my iPod and so listened to my music while Deano watched *Casino Royale* on his portable DVD player.

On the following morning, following an early breakfast, we left in coaches for the airstrip where we boarded a C-130 Hercules transport for the half-hour flight to Camp Bastion in Helmand.

Flying in a Hercules was an experience in itself. Strapped into our seats, we faced each other across the fuselage which was soon like an oven despite the crew leaving the rear ramp down a little. We had to keep all of our kit on, including our helmets, so our hair was soon clogged with sweat. The inevitable black humour soon surfaced, with one lad saying, 'What's the point in us wearing our helmets in this oven? It's not going to make a great deal of difference if we get hit in mid-air, plunging thousands of feet to our deaths.' He did have a point. In any case, our body armour was of the older type that only protected the area of the heart and, contrary to popular belief, did not stop the bullet. All it did was to ensure the exit wound would be the same size as the entry wound, so reducing the risk of the bullet creating a vacuum on impact and exiting about ten times the size, creating considerable internal damage.

In contrast, the new Osprey body armour was fantastic and we would be issued this within the first few days of arriving in Helmand. The Kevlar plates were huge and heavy but covered all of the vital organs and in ballistic tests proved that they could deflect a round from an AK-47, leaving only minor bruising. The vests that carry the plates are totally adaptable with nylon loops sewn on to the outside so you can attach magazine and utility pouches to it and not have to wear belt kit or a chest rig. Also on the back there are clips for attaching your water bottle and looping your drinking tube under your left arm so you can drink without taking your hands off of your weapon.

We approached Camp Bastion, an escort of Apache attack helicopters guiding us in during the last stage of our journey. Built in the middle of nowhere, in an area that is not too dissimilar to the fens in the east of England, Bastion appeared to be a safe place with the surrounding terrain being entirely flat for miles around, affording no cover for any form of conventional attack.

DEPLOYMENT

When we arrived, we found C Company about to move out for Kajaki in the north. A Company was needed to hold Nowzad while B Company was to look after Forward Operating Base (FOB) Robinson for two weeks. FOB Robinson's principal role was to provide artillery support for Sangin, which lay some six kilometres to the north and had seen some of the fiercest fighting in Afghanistan.

No sooner had had we arrived than we began our Reception, Staging & Onwards Integration (RSOI) package. This began with a series of briefings, studying local areas and analysing each attack that had taken place and numbers of enemy casualties, information on the Taliban and the kind of weapons they had been using and the various tactics being employed by them over the last period. We also underwent training on mines and mine clearance, and carried out a considerable amount of live firing with our weapons.

During this period, my fellow snipers and I made contact with our Royal Marine counterparts who provided us with a considerable amount of information including range data on the .338 calibre rifles we would be using. Once we had zeroed our weapons, we tested the Marines' range data out and it proved faultless at different ranges varying from a hundred metres up to a mile, enabling us to set up our rifles and telescopic sights ready for action.

CHAPTER 7

FOB Robinson

On completion of its RSOI package B Company, less No. 6 Platoon, received its initial orders for deployment. Attached to it would be its Fire Support Team (FST) which included mortar fire controllers (MFCs) and the Forward Air Controller (FAC) and his team who would call up air support if so required.

As I mentioned previously, FOB Robinson was situated around six kilometres south of Sangin. There was some Canadian artillery based there along with some of our own gunner units. We were to relieve the last group of 42 Royal Marine Commando there. 2nd Royal Tank Regiment (2 RTR) was due to move there but had not arrived at that time, so our orders were to deploy to FOB Robinson for two weeks before being relieved by 2 RTR who would be operating in the dismounted role, having left their Challenger 2 tanks at their home base in Wiltshire. After that, we were to be a Mobile Operations Group (MOG) while 2 RTR guarded the FOB and maintained security for the artillery providing fire support for Sangin and all the other out-stations in the area.

The advance party received orders to deploy by Chinook helicopter two days before the main force. I remember being issued our ammunition along with our personal medical kits which included two first field dressings (FFDs), a tourniquet, and a syrette of morphine. We had to carry ten litres of water, because water was in short supply in the FOB, in addition to the rest of our kit that comprised only essential items. All non-essential kit was stored in an ISO container for safekeeping while we were on operations.

We moved to the helicopter flight line on the Sunday morning. I was in the second group to move out and as we approached the flight line, the sheer weight of our kit became unbelievable, to the point where I could hear the stitching on our Bergens snapping open under the weight. Eventually, the packs began to give way under the strain, and so we arranged for a truck to take them up to the flight line. On arrival there, most of us needed help to don them again and stand up because we were wearing our full Osprey body armour with the big plates, which alone weighed 30 pounds, plus carrying a rifle weighing a further 9 pounds. This was in addition to ammunition, food, water, clothing, sleeping bag and everything else. I did keep my DVD player as my one luxury; it weighed nothing in comparison.

Aboard the Chinook, I sat looking out of the window as the helicopter rose gently and then lurched forwards before banking sharply to the left and beginning to climb, its blades thumping heavily. The tailgate was down, giving us a good view and allowing in air that became colder as we climbed higher.

After about ten minutes the aircraft dipped steeply as it manoeuvred itself down low into the Sangin Valley where, as we swept lower, I could see Afghan compounds for the first time, each of them in a form of a square with a box-like building in the centre. The loadmaster signalled to us to load our rifles and at that point I began to feel the butterflies in my stomach. This was it! This was when it really began to register in my mind that we were at war and this was no exercise! I was nervous as hell as we all inserted magazines into our rifles as we came low into the valley.

At that point the Chinook released a couple of flares with a loud thump while swerving from left to right while hugging the valley walls. The words 'Two minutes' came down the line, signalling that it was only two minutes until we landed. It seemed a long time. I am sure it was not only my heart that was racing, as we all knew what was happening. The front end of the helicopter rose up as it slowed down and flared for landing.

On disembarking from the Chinook, we ran as fast as possible through the dust clouds engulfing the whole scene before dropping to our knees about 50 metres from the helicopter. Looking back, I saw the loadmaster sprinting along with a number of Marines towards the aircraft, which took off a few moments later. All this lasted only around two minutes, but it seemed to be a lot longer as clouds of sand and stones sprayed over us. The reality was there were no mortars or shots being fired and it was actually a world apart from the visions I had in my head as we landed.

Colour Sergeant Snow, who was in command of my fire support group, FSG Bravo, was alongside Reedy and Bernie in a WMIK (weapons mount installation kit) which is a specially equipped Land Rover armed with a 7.62mm general purpose machine gun (GPMG) mounted forward in the commander's position and a .50 calibre heavy machine gun in the rear.

I walked over to the WMIK and dumped my kit on the back of the vehicle as Colour Sergeant Snow said, 'All right JC? Good flight?' My throat was dry because of the dust as I replied, 'Yeah Colour, I'm good. Where are we staying?' He pointed out a tower a little distance away and told me to go and find Pete Tointon who was second-in-command and, although a corporal, he was doing a sergeant's job. 'Go and see Pete and he'll square you away.'

Arriving in FOB Robinson, we learned that it consisted of two main parts: the tower and Snake Pit, and what we called the Dust Bowl that ran down to the 611 road. There was high ground to the east and west, which was called the Sangin Valley. Task Force Fury, an American unit was there. It was a typical American name and they did what the Americans do best, but it is tricky for me to talk about that.

I met up with Scotty and asked where Pete was and he replied that he was in the Snake Pit. When I asked what the hell the Snake Pit was, and was told that this was where the officers were based. Scotty showed me where our room, literally right next to a small room where the text link computer and a television were located. The computer had nothing else but the actual text link on it, not even a good game of solitaire. You typed in the mobile number of the phone to which you wanted to send a message and then the message which was sent as a text. Nice and simple and absolutely fantastic because I could send a text any time. We were four hours ahead, so I could wake up in the morning and send across a message to Annie. It operated on a similar basis to our mobile phones at home, where we were given around fifty credits per week and each text took around three credits. Like the telephone credits, these could be accumulated if you did not use them.

As we entered our room, Scotty said, 'Deano's on stag at the moment, your bed's there.' I opened a bottle of water and downed almost half of it. I noticed Scotty was wearing desert trousers and flip flops, so I stripped down to this as well, because I was absolutely soaked in sweat. Pete came in and was as cheerful as usual asking how I was, while I stood there almost out of breath from gulping the water too fast. At that point, my bergen arrived on the WMIK. Grabbing it, I brought it inside and then Scotty showed me around. It was just the four of us, Deano, Pete, Scotty and me, in this room as the rest of the FSG were in various compounds dotted around the Dust Bowl.

The whole place was somewhat gloomy, just brown everywhere, and looked as if it was basically made of mud and straw. The buildings were solid and sturdy, just like bricks and mortar, but most importantly stayed cool despite the stifling heat, the temperature inside never climbing above 10 degrees, providing much needed relief when we stepped in from over 40 degrees of heat outside.

The routine was simple. We got up, washed and cleaned our teeth, shaving not being mandatory due to the lack of water, and went on 'stag' when required to do so. We 'stagged on' with the FST up in the tower which controlled the artillery fire should it be required. There were also the FAC who controlled any air assets we had, which normally meant the Apache helicopters but every now and again US Air Force F-15 Eagles. In short, nothing happened at all in this first period of deployment. The whole area around us was mined, which meant we would not be conducting foot patrols; likewise, anyone attacking the FOB on foot would have had to tread very carefully. In the end, we organised it so snipers would stag on during the day, and the FST during the night but, at any time, twenty-four hours a day, the snipers would be on call to run to and man any of the positions needing assistance. If we needed to get 'eyes on' and fire a warning shot to let the enemy know we were there, or even if we needed to take a kill, we were on call whenever we were needed. Apart from us, the watchtowers were being manned by the rest of B Company, less No. 6 Platoon which was helping the Marines out with their last big operation.

B Company was preparing to go out on patrol and the FSG was to support it. Deano and Scotty were to be deployed while I was to take on all sniper duties in the FOB as I was now the only one left in the base because Teddy was still in the UK on his NCOs Cadre. If anyone saw anything suspicious I would have to leg it over to their position as quickly as possible.

We had received information, through various cast iron intelligence reports, that we were being watched at all times. The reports made us realise that the hills and valley of Sangin literally did have eyes. One night Sergeant Chris Canepa appeared in my room saying, 'Sniper needed at Sanger 8!' I sat up and was told that there were two Afghans digging next to a compound after last light and that it was suspected they could be planting a mine. All the locals around the FOB had been warned that would be considered a threat if seen digging after last light; in fact they had assured us that they do not farm at night. This meant that, under Rule 429 Alpha, we could engage if we thought they were Taliban or considered there was a possibility they had weapons or maybe were planting a mine.

I said, 'Okay, I'll be there in two!' I put my boots on, grabbed my kit and ran around to Sangar 8. One of the blokes, 'H' Holdenby, was in there with one of the other lads as I came in with a huge grin on my face. I was excited because this was my first opportunity to put into practice all my training, and to score my first hit. This may sound somewhat perverse, but it must be remembered that we were up against people trying to kill us and, if I was required to kill someone in the line of duty, I would not hesitate.

I switched on my night vision aid that clipped on to my rifle's telescopic sight. I remember the moon was not out, so visibility was poor. I had a target indication from 'H', but could not see the two targets. 'H' grabbed his 51mm light mortar and fired up a flare into the dark sky; as he did so I located the two Afghans with my laser rangefinder that gave me a bearing and range. They were standing in the gloom 460 metres away, so I dialled in 560 metres in to my scope elevation drum. I knew they were up to no good and was aware that someone had actually seen them digging, but they were now doing nothing. I realized that there was no way I could justify a kill, but I could and would give them a warning shot. I double-checked that I had dialled up the sight the extra 100 metres so the trajectory would take the bullet high, making an ear-splitting crack as it flew over their heads.

'H' launched a second flare and I aimed at the left-hand Afghan's face and fired, the bullet smashing into the wall behind him about three feet above his head. The man dropped to the ground and then both men ran off into the night, terrified out of their wits. I laughed, 'They won't be bothering you any more.' Gathering up my kit, I left the sangar and walked back up to the tower.

War tends to bring a mix of many emotions, sadness not least among them. The Battalion's first casualty was Private Chris Gray who died on 13 April 2007. I did not know him because he was from A Company with which I had never worked. Nevertheless, I was saddened because he looked like he was a young lad who had just recently joined the Army, and because he was a fellow soldier in the same regiment. Captain Robinson, the second-in-command of B Company, broke the news to us down in the Snake Pit.

A Company was deployed in the Green Zone in Nowzad, which was a bit of a ghost town with nothing of note there, but the problem it faced in the District Centre (DC) was that the Taliban were in strength there. The company could not move without being seen but, despite this, it had to push out and conduct patrols, knowing that the Taliban were everywhere. The Taliban used Nowzad as a rest area, using it to regroup after an operation before redeploying.

The company's task was to patrol, gain control of the ground and show the Taliban that it was in the area and would not tolerate any trouble. As it pushed into the Green Zone, the leading platoon had come under heavy fire and so Chris Gray's platoon moved around to execute a flanking manoeuvre to draw off some of the enemy fire. Chris Gray, as the lead man of the platoon, moved to within 20 metres of the Taliban position and engaged the enemy. A fierce fire fight ensued during which he was sadly hit in the chest. He was evacuated out of there, but died of his wounds later. Unfortunately, this is all I really knew of the incident, but it was a terrible shame and we all remembered this as the first casualty from our tour. Our thoughts went out to his family as we considered our own and the danger we were in during these moments of combat. It hit home to us that people would die out here, and we would be very naïve to think that we were somehow invincible. Each unit that had completed operational tours in this area had suffered casualties, but nevertheless we had to 'crack on' regardless.

Life at FOB Robinson continued, and I remember on one occasion being on stag up on the main FST tower, checking the area with binoculars. I noticed the Americans were there and that they also had their snipers up on the roofs. I observed an American patrol moving between some of the buildings below the snipers' positions and then suddenly saw and heard a massive explosion next to them, with dust and debris being thrown up high in to the air. I got on to the field telephone to the Ops Room, describing what I had seen in the American area. It transpired that one of their number had stepped on a mine, in all probability an old Russian mine replanted by the Taliban.

Amongst these hills there was an ancient old fort that reputedly dated back to Alexander the Great's time. It was on a small hill and you can see it was obviously man-made, but it had melted into the terrain over time. The Taliban reportedly used to fire from it so I always used to keep an eye on the area of the fort when on stag. The FOB had not come under serious attack from small arms, just mortars and 107mm Chinese rockets, but a couple of mortar bombs came towards us, although we were only there for a few weeks. So, apart from a few mortar bombs, not a great deal happened during the few weeks we were there. Generally speaking, life in FOB Robinson was actually pretty boring. It would become the epitome of luxury in comparison to what we would experience in due course. The main source of annoyance was the Canadian artillery that had a habit of loosing off salvoes while I was in bed, the noise rendering sleep impossible.

Otherwise, we did have the satellite phones that were like big mobile phones with large antennas that worked on the same card that you could use on the landlines in Camp Bastion. This gave me the opportunity of speaking to Annie, which was great, because she always sounded so excited and really glad to hear my voice. This, coupled with receiving letters was really good for morale and always boosted mine a hell of a lot. I also sent text messages to her through the text link often and this also helped keep her in the loop.

Eventually, the time came for us to leave FOB Robinson. Teddy had arrived and was waiting for us in Camp Bastion, having passed his lance corporal cadre. While the FSG drove back in the WMIKs it had acquired from FOB Robinson, the snipers were flown back by Chinook along with Nos. 5 and 7 Platoons.

CHAPTER 8

Operation SILICONE and HBK

O n arriving back at Camp Bastion, we found that we were based in Pod B, Camp 501, within the main camp itself. 6 Platoon was already in action and was still in Gereshk manning FOB Price and carrying out patrols around the area. B Company was equipped with Viking vehicles, which were absolutely fantastic and without doubt the best vehicles for crossing desert terrain. Modular in design, they could be coupled together like a train. The forward or 'cab' element of the vehicle was equipped to accommodate four men, together with a platform for a gunner armed with a 7.62mm with a GPMG mounted in a rotating turret.

The ultimate all-terrain high mobility vehicle, the Viking runs on rubber tracks which do not sink into the sand. It is also very fast and, equally importantly, very good when coming into contact with mines. If it runs over a standard type of anti-tank mine, everyone inside would be shaken up but would survive up while the vehicle would still be capable of being driven away. The Taliban employed a tactic to try to counter this by stacking two or three mines on top of each other but, although this would immobilise the Viking, those inside still stood a good chance emerging unscathed. The modular aspect of the vehicles afforded a lot of space and you could fire out of the back from a top-cover hatch. Inside the vehicle, it would be incredibly hot, with the temperature sometimes approaching 40 or 50 degrees. Some of the Vikings were equipped with air conditioning which was a godsend when it worked.

On arriving at Camp Bastion, I called my mum and Annie to tell them to post everything to me there as the move from FOB Robinson was complete. At about this time I began receiving parcels from everyone, which was really good and excellent for morale. In addition to this, Teddy turned up and it was great to see him and there was a lot of smiles and backslapping. Deano had been trying to get us issued with pistols as he was in command, but it was just not happening. I guess someone did not want the snipers swaggering around with pistols, but in fact we really did need them. If, for example, we went into the Green Zone and encountered a group of Taliban with AK-47's at close range, we would have been in serious trouble as we only had bolt action .338 sniper rifles that only hold five rounds in the magazine. We were eventually successful, our argument being that if we were moving through alleyways or around buildings, we needed to have our pistols drawn so that we could react quickly and effectively to a threat at close quarters.

We came across the sniper team for A Company that consisted of Jock who was in command, with Donny as second-in-command, and JL and OB as the two shooters. It was great to see them, especially considering the snipers had not been together as a platoon since February. OB told us about the big contact in Nowzad, which I think was the same one in which Chris Gray unfortunately got killed. He said that they had been in amongst the buildings when it happened, and had to climb up on to the roofs to enable them to observe. As they did so, they came under heavy fire. Realising they were needed to give fire support and would have to push forward, they decided to split up into pairs. Running through a series of seemingly endless alleyways OB, with Jock behind him, turned a corner and came face to face with a Taliban fighter. Fortunately, he had his pistol in his hand and reacted swiftly, firing the entire magazine of thirteen rounds into the fighter who opened fire at the same time with his AK-47. OB hit him three times around the shoulder area while fortunately escaping completely unscathed. The fighter disappeared around a corner out of sight, so OB threw a grenade after him. Later, he discovered that his pistol had a groove exactly 7.62mm wide along the length of the top slide. When he told us this, there was a chorus of, 'You lucky bastard!' and he had indeed been extremely fortunate. The fighter was hit three times but still managed to run off. It was widely rumoured at the time that quite a few of the Taliban were high on heroin, which would have helped to numb pain. This was never proven, but there were several of us who experienced Taliban running at us wildly and continuing to move despite sustaining serious injury.

We spent most of the following week on the range or in the Skills House, which was a mock-up of the type of compound you would find in the Afghan desert, Green Zone or any other occupied area. In the western world you would typically have a detached house with a white picket fence and driveway, but an Afghan house was normally a walled compound with iron gates, usually painted green or blue, that were wide enough for a car to pass through. In the middle of most compounds, you would normally have a patch of dirt with various plants such as poppies growing, but the buildings themselves were just square and built out of mud and straw with flat roofs. Unlike in the UK, they had stairs on the outside but basically were square boxes attached to each other.

Bizarrely, these constructions, ancient in their design and simplicity, were actually better at stopping our bullets or grenades than modern brick houses and, although solid, could also flex and move. For example, if we tried firing a 40mm grenade from an underbarrel grenade launcher (UGL) fitted to an SA80, it would hit and either bounce off or simply embed itself in the wall and fail to explode. So we had to adapt our tactics accordingly, firing to hit the ground in front of them instead.

The Skills House was an accurate mock-up, albeit made from wood and hessian, and we would use it to practise tactics such as room clearance, with the positions of the twelve or so targets inside being changed each time. We would then have a debrief where we would go through any mistakes. It was fantastic training which gave you a hell of an adrenalin rush, because you forgot that it was not for real and took it dead seriously. We needed to change and adapt our fighting style to counter the enemy effectively and we had to learn fast. This was where we did it, in the Skills House and on the ranges.

Snipers were usually being deployed with the FSG on the flanks, but both Deano and I realised that this would be no good if the company went into the Green Zone, which is where the Helmand River runs down from Kajaki to the south of the province. Along either side of the river, to a depth of one kilometre, are areas populated by the local people who grow poppies for opium or crops such as maize or corn. We knew that we could not hang back and clinically remove targets at long range; we had no choice but to go in with the rifle platoons.

During this period of training, Teddy and I were very nearly wiped out by friendly fire. In the Skills House, the guys were reacting to some machine gun fire and we decided that we would not actually enter the compound, but move to the right flank and observe for any enemy in depth or running away from the compound. So, while the guys were firing and manoeuvring forward, we had moved from behind them and on to the right hand flank of the compound, taking up our new position as quickly as possible.

At this point there were no proper targets set out, so we had to make do with random piles of dirt and blocks of Hesco-Bastion which comprises steel cages lined with canvas and filled with dirt, a very easy and effective way of building walls or structures. We went through the normal procedure, with me using my laser rangefinders to 'zap' a target and thereafter giving Teddy the range and wind details for him to engage it. We would both observe the target and then he would fire. We repeated this process with between five and ten targets. It was invaluable practice in understanding each other and being able to second guess what we were both thinking all the time. Using the invaluable data the Marines had given us, coupled with using the rangefinders along with the fantastic .338 rifle, Teddy scored ten out of ten, which boosted our confidence enormously.

The only problem was that, as we were engaging our targets, we suddenly heard a whistling sound followed by a thud about ten metres behind us. I spun around to see a white smouldering plume of smoke. We then heard a thump in the distance, followed again by the whistling sound and another smoking plume about 30 metres away on the ground to our left.

The mortar man – OUR OWN mortar man – was firing live smoke behind us! I grabbed the radio and called him up, '51 mortar, you are engaging friendly snipers with your smoke. Check your fire! Check fire! Friendly snipers in smoked area.' To our relief, we received the immediate response, 'Roger, checking fire.' The reason it was so critical for us to make contact was that the mortars always fired smoke first to gauge the fall of shot before firing high explosive (HE) bombs. If I had not heard or noticed the smoke bombs landing around us, the mortars would have switched to HE and Teddy and I would have been dead. At least we now knew the sound of an incoming friendly mortar!

Shortly afterwards, Snowy briefed us on Operation SILICONE which would begin on 29 April and continue until 8 May. It seemed fairly straightforward, with us being split into two groups, one sniper team north and one south. Teddy and I would be in the north while Deano and Scotty deployed in the south.

The area in which it would take place was called Habibollah Kalay, known to all of us as HBK. One rifle company was to sweep from west to east through HBK with the northern FSG mounted in Vikings. Mick and a guy called OD, a Territorial who had joined us for the tour, would go in on foot with a man-packed Javelin missile system together with the FST which would control all the air and mortar support were also there.

SILICONE's objective was the clearing of a known stronghold of the Taliban north east of Gereshk. With eleven sub-units under command, including our A and B Companies, it was an ambitious, large scale operation and the first time a clearance of this scale had been attempted within the Green Zone. B Company would lead the way with A Company in support. Once the area had been cleared of Taliban, three patrol bases would be sited and constructed from which patrolling would be conducted to deny the area to the enemy.

A change was made to our order of battle (Orbat). This irritated me because Teddy was put in command of a WMIK and there was no room for us in the Viking with the FST. So, for the first day of the operation, I would basically be redundant because the WMIKs provided vehicle-mounted fire support and so there would not be much scope for me to dismount and do anything. This meant that I was relegated to sitting in the back of the vehicle on top of a load of boxes of ammunition, which was the most uncomfortable journey of my life.

On the day the operation began, we left Camp Bastion and drove off into the desert with me in the back of the WMIK being bounced around, cursing every time my shins got smashed against the metal ammunition boxes. Eventually we halted for the night, the vehicles forming a circle facing outwards in 'all round defence', ready to push on before first light on the following day. I remember looking out in to the pitch darkness and hearing the sound of the wind increasing, almost like a shock wave growing in its intensity and pitch. Suddenly, we all realized that we were caught in the middle of a sandstorm. I grabbed my sleeping bag with all my might, holding on to it with both hands as sand flew around us. I tried to peer out through slitted eyes but received an eyeful of sand, so squeezed them tight shut and turned my back on the brunt of the storm. It felt as though someone was playing a power washer hose on it, but using sand instead of water. The sandstorm lasted for only around thirty seconds, and then everything was still. Once it stopped, we opened our eyes to see people chasing after sleeping bags and roll mats. At around 3.00 or 4.00 am, this was a somewhat bizarre sight in the middle of the desert.

On arriving at the forming up point (FUP), I transferred to the Viking with the FST. It was not long before our troops came under heavy fire in the Green Zone and the FST was directing aircraft in to drop ordinance. The Apache attack helicopters in support of us were very reluctant to attack any compounds without proper confirmation of Taliban occupation. They were being cautious because our own guys were now actually in the Green Zone where they were coming under very heavy fire. As they tried to move forward they came under fire from another compound nearby which they initially thought was a school. The Taliban were firing automatic weapons out of every window of each compound and our guys were pinned down in desperate need of air support in order to regain the initiative and maintain momentum.

While the Apaches were hesitating, the Americans had overheard on radio transmissions and, having been given the coordinates, swept in and dropped a 1,000lb Joint Defence Attack Munition (JDAM) directly onto the target.

While this was going on, I looked across and noticed another Viking vehicle. Running across to it, I discovered the air conditioning was on which was just total bliss. It was the beginning of May now and the temperatures ranged from the mid-forties in the day to the mid-twenties at night, which is a nightmare to sleep in. I was just about to jump into it when Teddy called over from his WMIK and asked me if I wanted to use my .338. With that, I grabbed my rifle and ammunition and mounted the empty Viking. Standing up through the top hatch, I was observing a group of small buildings when an RPG (rocket propelled grenade) whizzed past me. Everyone returned fire with various weapons, including .50 cal heavy machine guns. The enemy responded with a few bursts but we maintained the pressure by keeping them under a heavy volume of fire. RPGs are nasty because they spread shrapnel all over the place when they impact, and so can be really deadly.

The Taliban continued launching RPGs at us, one after another. Whenever we saw the dust that flew up from where they were launched, we concentrated our fire on those locations. Just as Pete spotted a window from which some of the RPGs were coming, one flew past about 5 metres above my head. I dropped as deep as I could into the vehicle as it exploded behind us, the blast making our bodies shudder. Pete launched a Javelin missile and scored a direct hit. This slowed the enemy fire down considerably but there were still the odd few cracks of rounds flying past us.

This continued with fire being put down by both sides for another ten minutes or so. Another RPG flew over the top of 'Strikey's' WMIK bonnet just as he was shouting, 'Over there! Reference that building with three windows, next to the tallest building!' I 'zapped' it with my rangefinder, pinpointing the target at 628 metres. I took into account the wind aspect while thinking, 'This is it!' My heart was racing as I aimed and took up the first pressure on the trigger. There was an incredibly bright flash as yet another RPG left that particular window and I immediately put two rounds in quick succession directly into it. I will never know if I killed the man with the RPG, but the firing ceased immediately. I guess he had either been hit and was now dead or I missed and he made good his escape, living to fight another day. Either way, the job was done and the threat neutralised.

The company cleared the built up area and we moved around to pick it up. All the guys had been 'in contact' with the enemy for around twelve hours and were completely exhausted. The most gratifying aspect of the operation for all of us was that the objective had been achieved without incurring any casualties. It was estimated that there were around ninety-five enemy dead, so the operation was deemed a great success.

Morale was really very high, but we had to stay professional and disciplined because we now had to move to Phase 2 and defend against the inevitable counterattacks. This phase of the operation would last for at least a week and became known as the battle of HBK. In the meantime we occupied three compounds in the area, each platoon establishing a defended base from which to deploy patrols.

All the snipers, two WMIKS and two Vikings helped 7 Platoon man its compound. Three permanent vehicle checkpoints were to be built nearby and a further three bases, designated north, central and south, to be established and manned by the Afghan National Army (ANA). We set out claymore mines and tripflares around the area and blasted down some of the trees to open up the arcs of fire. I recall there were poppies as far as the eye could see, and cannabis plants dotted around all the canals and drainage ditches.

At this stage in the operation, we received information that sixty Taliban fighters were now in the area and attempting to surround our position. The tension rose as we busied ourselves filling sandbags and carrying them to various points, including up ladders on to the roofs to build up our defences. In the event, nothing happened. We stagged on day and night while continuing to fill more sandbags, digging out the earth from the compound's garden in the intense heat. At the same time, we were also felling trees to prevent the Taliban from climbing up them or using them as cover.

All the while, we poured with sweat as we toiled away improving the defences of our base. One of the new guys, a young lad called Troy, was clearly suffering quite badly from heat exhaustion, so I let Parky, his section commander, know. He asked me to keep an eye on him, so I sat with Troy and gave him some water, made sure he was in the shade and kept him talking while generally making sure he was all right. He was a really good bloke who would remain a friend.

As I mentioned, nothing happened that first day apart from stagging on. All we really saw, as we continued working on our defences, were civilians and farmers leaving the area as they had clearly been warned to expect a battle. On the second night at around two in the morning, we heard gunfire in the distance and saw the odd tracer flying skywards. The PVCP-North (Permanent Vehicle Check Point) was under attack attacked and the mortars were putting up illumination flares. Amazingly, the ANA troops manning the checkpoint stood their ground and repelled the attack.

On the following day, we were tasked with patrolling the area to ensure that it was safe for the CSM (Company Sergeant Major) to bring in food and water. We received a load of 'Menu B' rations which were not one of my favourites, but I tended to spread my melted Yorkie bars over the biscuits. To be honest, the heat tended to sap away my appetite anyway, and we had more to worry about because over the next few nights, the Taliban mounted attacks in the north and central areas. These often only lasted half an hour or so and seemed more like probing attacks.

One morning, an Afghan local approached the compound with his hands in the air. I made sure I had 'eyes on him' with my rifle. As he came up to the main area, I could see that he was an older man, maybe fifty years of age. I still had my telescopic sight trained on him but could see no sign of weapons or any evidence of anything being concealed under his robes, so I shouted down to the platoon commander for the interpreter. It transpired that the compound we were occupying belonged to this man and he wished to return later with his two sons to pick up some belongings.

Sure enough, that afternoon, they appeared and started to pull up their robes to show that they were not suicide bombers. This was a drill that the Paras had instilled into them, so we did not even have to ask them to do this. They were allowed into the compound where they began putting clothes and personal effects into bags. The old man then began to dig in an area of the poppy field. Teddy watched him carefully, his hand on his pistol in case he produced a weapon, but eventually he pulled out a yellow bucket. The interpreter asked the old man what it contained and he announced that it was opium, peeling off the lid to show the golden brown colour of pure opium ready to be turned into heroin. As one of the sons walked over with another bucket, the interpreter told us that this bucket would feed his family for an entire year.

The opium would be sold for $1,000 to a drug baron, who would in turn sell it on for around $10,000. It would eventually end up as street heroin worth around $100,000 and be bought by 'smack heads' in the West. It is the heroin and lucrative drugs trade that funds the Taliban, with ninety per cent of the heroin in the UK coming from Afghanistan. We had to watch this trade going on around us, but were not allowed to take any action against the drug barons or stop the opium production. To do so before better alternatives could be offered to the farmers would have wrecked the local economy and acted as a recruiting sergeant for the Taliban.

We remained in the area for another week and with our support the ANA continued successfully to repel attacks, enabling us at the same time to get ready to leave. After a few more days spent patrolling, we withdrew and handed over to the 1st Battalion The Worcestershire & Sherwood Foresters Regiment.

CHAPTER 9

Mobile Operations

On returning from Operation SILICONE, we began to prepare ourselves to deploy on Mobile Operation Groups (MOGs). A and C Companies were based at Nowzad and Kajaki where they defended and patrolled their respective areas. C Company's presence at Kajaki was due to the hydro-electric dam there. Although running at less than half of its capacity, it still supplied electricity to many thousands of people within the Sangin Valley. The British had not only promised the Afghan government to protect the dam, but also to return it to full capacity in order to supply the entire valley with electricity. The dam tapped into Helmand River, which runs straight through the province of Helmand where the majority of the villages are located near the river.

C Company's task was to push the Taliban away from the area of the dam. Meanwhile, B Company and its FSG would deploy from Camp Bastion in Viking vehicles manned by Royal Marines. Our task was to move into the desert near the Green Zone, and specifically target the various villages and compounds that were under Taliban influence or control, driving out the enemy and returning the villages to the locals. The first of these was called Pasab. After the success of Operation SILICONE and HBK, we were looking forward to the Pasab operation, brimming with confidence and ready to take on the world. Deano had managed to talk B Company's commander, Major Mick Aston, into allowing the snipers to be attached to the platoons instead of staying with the WMIK fire support vehicles. During Operation SILICONE and HBK, Teddy was commanding a WMIK while I had attempted to snipe out of a Viking, which had not worked well. Deano and his team, on the other hand, had actually been in the Green Zone with the platoons, providing surveillance and a supporting fire role, which proved very effective. We were going to have to try a whole new way of sniping for which we had not trained previously, so would literally be learning on the job.

Teddy and I packed our kit, although there was only a limited amount we could realistically take. To solve the problem we decided to share a Bergen between us, this being strapped to the side of the Viking carrying 7 Platoon, which was commanded by Lieutenant George Seal-Coon, with Sergeant Woodrow as the platoon sergeant. The brilliant thing about these two was that they did not try to control us, allowing us to carry out our tasks in our own way. I carried a radio to maintain communications with the platoon and Major Aston. This proved to be a perfect arrangement, allowing us to report not only where we were but also what we could see. The role of snipers is not just the clinical removal of targets, but also observation and provision of information on the enemy. As we soon found out, the Taliban do not simply sit still and shoot, but are quick to use flanking manoeuvres and engaged us with tactics that needed spotting early. The number one priority of a sniper is usually to target an officer or someone who is obviously in command. The Taliban, of course, wear no distinguishing insignia so our targeting was instead based on threat, with those seen to be equipped with RPGs or machine guns receiving priority over those armed with an AK-47 or a pistol.

Leaving Camp Bastion, we headed across the desert towards Pasab, a small village on the edge of the Green Zone. A large canal ran along the far end of the village, along which we were to patrol keeping a close eye on the far side of it. If possible, we were to cross it and patrol up to the Helmand River, clearing the area right up to the river itself. As usual whenever we appeared, all the locals began to flee the area in a hurry. This was a pretty good indicator that the Taliban were there and waiting. We just had to find out how many and where.

There was a Bedouin camp to the south of Pasab. The people in these camps were referred to as 'sand pikeys' because they were desert nomads. We were to bypass the camp as it was not part of the village, the built-up area of Pasab being our main objective. We were observing a local on a moped who kept driving at speed across the front of our arc at a range of about 600 metres in front of us. We watched him closely whenever he stopped, trying to identify any weapons on him. We could not see any but were suspicious he was the only inhabitant remaining in the area while the remainder were all heading away as quickly as possible. I reported this over the radio, voicing our suspicions that he was estimating our strength, and received the response, 'Give him a warning shot.'

I gave Teddy the range data and checked the wind as he dialled it into his scope. I used my rangefinder to 'zap' a junction in the dirt track, along which the local was heading, to give an exact distance. As the moped approached to within 10 metres of the junction, Teddy fired. The round whizzed past in front of the moped, the sudden shock almost making the local fall off. Teddy grinned and we high fived as the local sped off into the distance.

We patrolled across the open area with 5 Platoon, to which Deano and Scotty were attached, in support. Teddy and I were with Corporal Martin's section, which was in the lead. When we crossed open ground, we moved in just behind the lead section. That way we had some protection from the rear and also from the front, so from whichever direction the contact took place we would be in the middle of the platoon.

As we moved on, an old man came out from the Bedouin camp shouting and waving his arms furiously. I later found out from one of the interpreters that he was politely telling us to, 'Go home, or die.' Some really horribly malnourished dogs skirted round us in packs of five or six, snarling and growling. Some of them were foaming at the mouth and were really just skin and bone, with matted fur and bald areas covered in scars.

We eventually reached the village, and then made our way through buildings and meandering compounds. The loudest thing for me was the silence, reminding me of scenes from spaghetti westerns with tumbleweed rolling along empty streets. We moved on and patrolled through, looking into doorways, but the whole area seemed utterly deserted.

All of a sudden a shot rang out and everyone took cover, those in the open slamming themselves into the ground. Teddy and I dived behind a crumbling wall, dropping to our knees and observing around us. I listened to the radio as the tension mounted until we heard someone shout out, 'It's all right! A dog went for me, so I dropped it.'

We stood up and dusted ourselves off before continuing to patrol forward and clear the village unopposed. Eventually we reached the canal, which was sunken with high banks on either side, so much so that it was hard to tell you had reached it until you were right on top of it. Close to where Teddy and I halted was a large building with big green double doors.

Suddenly, out of nowhere, there was a sudden and prolonged burst of machine gun fire directly above our heads. We scrambled for cover and I could see that it was coming from the far side of the canal. Corporal Martin gave his section a fire control order and started to suppress the fire. Meanwhile, Corporal Parker and his section moved up to a compound to the left, Teddy and I following them into a building from which we began observing the thick treeline from where the fire had come. The canal swept round from left to right quite steeply, curving away from us towards a steep mound on the other side. Beyond were thick woods and really dense treelines in which it was almost impossible to observe any movement.

The area was dotted with compounds, some of them 6 or 7 feet in height while others were only waist high. We had tucked ourselves into a compound with walls of around 4 or 5 feet in height, so we could see over the top and shoot out. The treeline was only around 50 metres away, and the noise was unbelievable. My heart was racing and my mouth was dry as the enemy kept up a heavy volume of fire, even launching a couple of RPGs at us, one exploding about 20 metres to my right, its shockwave actually making my teeth rattle. Teddy opened fire with his rifle into a small building next to an old footbridge which spanned canal, while 5 Platoon moved up to support us. To prevent us all from becoming bunched into one compound, Corporal Parker's section went through a small doorway that led to a gap between more compounds. This ended up in an area that had high sandbanks leading up to the canal and the section spread itself along one of them, engaging the treeline while trying to locate any likely enemy fire positions. There was a small hut just off to the left of a small footbridge about 200 to 300 metres away and I began to fire directly into that area, while observing the treeline and trying to pinpoint a definite target. The volume of fire and the denseness of cover were such that it was really very difficult to locate the enemy.

Teddy had joined Corporal Parker's section while I attached myself to Corporal Martin's, positioning myself to protect the flank. I knelt down next to a building but as I did so the wall above my head exploded in a cloud of dust and debris as a continual hail of bullets flew literally inches above my head. I lay flat on the floor almost willing the earth to open up and allow me to get lower, even just a few more inches to give me cover. I then started to crawl as fast as I could, eventually reaching a doorway where I managed to gather myself a bit. One of the 5 Platoon lads had seen it all happen and began returning the enemy fire. While he was doing that, I looked back around the corner and about a metre away there was just a big piece of wall totally mashed up where the fire had been thumping into it.

At this point I decided to find out where Corporal Martin was and tell him that there were enemy attempting to outflank us to the right, and that one of them had spotted me and pretty much emptied a magazine at me. I then met up with Teddy and Corporal Parker's section as 5 Platoon moved up on our left flank and came under heavy fire from the enemy. It became apparent that the enemy were moving up from the other side of the canal against the steep bank, which was why we could not see them. They had been popping up on the other side of this bank, firing over from only around 50 metres away then getting back down and scurrying back off. By now they had moved right along the canal and spotted 5 Platoon, and started to lay down more heavy fire.

We called up a fire mission over the radio for our mortars to finish off any of the Taliban on that part of the canal, quickly taking up positions so we were at a safe distance from the bombs. We were observing the treeline when Corporal Parker spotted the enemy and shouted, 'There's one in the trees! Rapid fire, rapid fire!.' Private John Thrumble responded with his GPMG, accompanied by six others with their SA80s, while Teddy also joined in with his .338, a heavy volume of fire smashing into the treeline. We all watched as a limp, lifeless body fell out of the trees and thumped to the ground on the other side of the canal. Thereafter, we continued firing and launched a number of 40mm grenades, fired from underbarrel grenade launchers (UGLs), into the area. A hand grenade was thrown by one of our number but it had no effect as it struck the bank on the far side before rolling down and exploding in the canal, showering us with water.

The message came through that we were moving back for a 'pick up.' It was decided that we could not cross the river, because there was only really one main crossing point provided by a rickety old wooden bridge and that would have been suicidal to use. So the call was made for the canal area to be bombarded by the mortars while we pulled out of there. We could hear them in the distance beginning to fire. They called each pair of mortars with a number. For example, if the distance and trajectory was going to take fifteen seconds from point of firing to point of impact, it was called, 'Shot one five.' When you consider we were only around 50 metres away from the Taliban and were already beginning to hear our mortars being fired in quick succession, you can see why we really needed to pull out fast.

As we moved away, we cleared a compound by firing into it and throwing grenades in through doorways. We also threw smoke grenades and ran through the smoke while continuing to withdraw. The enemy fire died down to almost nothing as we heard our own mortar bombs whistling down and impacting on the other side of the canal, explosion after explosion after explosion. We were 'tabbing' at a fast pace and I can remember being incredibly pumped up as the adrenalin flowed.

As we stopped by a dried-up river bed, the vehicles appeared. We were sharing ours with some of the combat engineers led by a big fat Welsh corporal. One of the sappers was of Asian appearance, similar to a Gurkha, and next to him was a very pale-skinned Jock with ginger hair. They watched wide-eyed as we piled in and ripped off our helmets, pouring with sweat and gulping water like madmen as we swapped accounts of the action. We talked fast, wondering if others had spotted the body falling out of the tree or me nearly getting my head blown off and other things like this as we began to pull away. Unfortunately our vehicle didn't have air conditioning, so every time we stopped we threw the back door open and gulped at the air, before having to close it again as we continued. On reaching the open desert, we halted and set up all-round defence. This was our first patrol on MOGs and it had certainly proved to be eventful.

The next village we were scheduled to patrol was a place called Zumberlay. The Marines we relieved had told us that they had been involved in a lengthy action there, scoring quite a number of kills.

After a night's rest, we replenished our ammunition and water supplies and drove back into the Sangin Valley. This time we entered it slightly further to the north, dismounting on some high ground over to the east of Zumberlay and receiving a set of quick battle orders. The plan was to break into the village and then push north-west to the limit of exploitation, the furthest point up to which we were permitted to advance. The FSG was staying on the high ground to cover us, so we dismounted and 5 Platoon, which was to take the lead on this particular patrol, prepared for battle.

I saw Deano and Scotty and gave them a thumbs-up just as the last man of 5 Platoon disappeared into the dead ground while Teddy, I and 7 Platoon advanced to the ridge to give fire support. We were moving up when we heard a massive explosion as an RPG whistled overhead and impacted some 200 metres behind us. We ran forward to start observing and shots rang out as 5 Platoon engaged the enemy. Meanwhile Deano and Scotty scrambled up on to a compound roof. Another RPG was launched at us, exploding behind us but closer this time as the Taliban began to find their range. We could hear the FSG beginning to fire Javelin missiles but could not see anything until we saw a compound literally blown to pieces, which sent us whooping and giving high fives.

5 Platoon continued pushing forward and the firing ceased as 7 Platoon moved along the same route in and pushed around to the left to give flank protection. After about the seventh compound, as we reached a wide open road and began to cross, 5 Platoon halted and gave us cover as we moved forward with Major Aston to meet the commander of 5 Platoon. We looked at the different possible approaches and decided to parallel each other on either side of the road.

Teddy and I then took up a position on a roof to provide over-watch. Corporal Parker's section was going to be the first into the compounds, accompanied by a combat engineer equipped with a bar-mine. Originally designed for use against tanks, we were using them to blow large holes, known as 'mouseholes', in the walls of compounds to gain entry. The shock wave from an exploding bar mine is phenomenal. I was always told to close my eyes and open my mouth so that the air in your lungs can escape through your mouth to avoid any risk of internal damage. The trouble was, if you opened your mouth too wide you would get a mouth full of dust, debris and God knows what else. On the other hand, if you didn't open it enough, your teeth would whack together so hard it really hurt.

The 'mousehole' was blown and Corporal Parker's section burst into the compound, bayonets fixed, firing rounds and throwing a few grenades as they went in, not taking any chances because the enemy could have been in any of the compounds we were clearing. Luckily this one was clear, so Sergeant Woodrow launched Corporal Martin's section with Teddy and I following up behind. It was a big compound, but empty apart from dead poppies.

Teddy climbed on to a flimsy roof while I stayed on the ground as we did not want to risk falling through it. Although we needed to position ourselves on these roofs to obtain the best possible vantage points, some of them were made of solid mud and straw while others were just straw, so we had to be careful. The rest of 7 Platoon came in and took up positions to give us our own defence. We had air support in the form of a Harrier on station, so Major Aston halted us to give the pilot a chance to try to find the enemy from above or for our FAC to give him targets to engage. After about ten minutes the pilot reported that he could not see anything moving, so he had decided to carry out a 'show of force' – a low-level pass over the area. Teddy tossed me his camera and I succeeded in filming the aircraft as it hurtled in at treetop height, the roar from its engines deafening us below.

As the Harrier flew away, 5 and 7 Platoons continued north to Zumberlay. We were totally unopposed as we patrolled but knew we were being watched. We did not take any chances, sprinting when crossing open spaces and zigzagging to make ourselves difficult targets. Eventually we completed the task and called for a pick-up by our Vikings which appeared at the edge of the village where we mounted up with still no sound from the enemy.

We drove back out to the desert and the company spent the next few days patrolling various villages in the area, but nothing of any note really happened, apart from a couple of contacts similar to that at Zumberlay. Each time, we were reaching our objectives and pushing the Taliban further up the Sangin Valley. Although we had not taken any casualties, that was all about to change.

We returned to Camp Bastion and after a few days were told to pack our kit for a three-day operation. This time we were to patrol and clear a village called Tsawmishi, which was known to have a large number of Taliban, so we knew from the start that we could be in for a really hard fight. Tsawmishi lies to the south of a sharp bend in the river Helmand which forms an inverted 'V' with its apex facing north. To the north of the river, spanned by an old bridge, is a village called Hyderabad.

The following day found us on the high ground looking over Tsawmishi with the bridge as our objective. Entering from the east, 5 Platoon was to lead and push towards the compounds on the right-hand side where it would halt and go firm. 7 Platoon would then push through before 5 Platoon and cross the open ground into the left-hand side of the western area and push north through the compounds towards the bridge. The compounds ran parallel to the river, eventually joining up at the bridge; at the largest point there was a large, wide expanse of land about a kilometre wide. A well populated area, it also contained some treelines and vegetation although not as dense as those we had encountered previously.

The first platoon to reach the bridge was to capture it and hold it, while the other headed back towards the south to provide protection for the elders of the community. This was commonly known as a 'shura', a council of elders who controlled the whole area. In the Afghan culture, people are very respectful of their elders and part of our mission was not only to protect them, but also listen to them and explain the reasons for our presence. We had to win the hearts and minds of the locals while also hopefully gaining valuable information about the enemy.

5 Platoon, accompanied by Deano and Scotty, set off with us following along with 7 Platoon, the approach route taking us through poppy fields and drainage ditches. As soon as 5 Platoon reached the first of the compounds, it came under fire. We listened to the radio net as we ran forward 600 or 700 metres through fields and around corners of buildings. The enemy were bringing heavy fire to bear from automatic weapons and RPGs, and it was clear to us that we needed to move forward so that if the platoons mounted an attack we could move to a flank and provide effective supporting fire.

5 Platoon was returning fire and holding the compounds as 7 Platoon ran forward through some patchy wooded areas. Teddy and I were just behind the lead section and by the time we caught up with 5 Platoon the shooting had died down. By that stage, the platoon commander had decided to close in on the enemy who appeared to be withdrawing to the north. In the meantime, 7 Platoon regrouped in a wadi.

We then began to come under enemy mortar fire. There was that dreaded whistling sound as the bombs fell. It gets louder and louder until there is about a half-second pause before the bombs explodes and you see the grains of sand in front of you shudder and jump off the ground while the shock wave swamps you, shaking you until your teeth rattle. We all got down as low as possible to protect ourselves from shrapnel and pieces of flying rock.

One of the bombs exploded about 100 metres to my right and this was followed immediately by shouts of, 'Man down! Man down!' We all spread out as the mortar fire got closer and closer. The medic, we called him Macca, sprinted past us towards the injured man, Corporal Martin, who had a really deep laceration in his arm caused by shrapnel. At this point an American aircraft swooped in out of nowhere and fired on the enemy position, followed by another that dropped a 1,000 pound JDAM bomb on the main enemy-held compound.

The enemy mortar fire ceased and 5 Platoon now moved forward, covered by 7 Platoon. Our FSG hammered the left-hand side of the compound near the ridge as 5 Platoon moved across the open ground towards the enemy positions, doubling across the open. Teddy and I meanwhile clambered up on to a roof and began to observe the compounds. Deano and Scotty were in with 5 Platoon and gave sniper cover for their guys as we continued moving north. We encountered small pockets of enemy resistance, but they were largely not interested in holding their ground. Instead it appeared they were retreating back towards the bridge, which they held in strength, clearly intending to make a proper stand there.

We had now been involved in this contact for a few hours and the engineers were blowing mouseholes in the walls of the compounds so we could enter. There are three codes when entering a building. Red is to throw grenades in first and then enter firing whether you see enemy or not; Amber is to go in with just your weapon and without grenades; and green is to enter without either. On this occasion, we initially were going in red each time, throwing grenades and laying down fire. As the battle continued, we dropped or raised the code depending on the threat as we saw it, because if we continued through on code Red throughout we would be in danger of running out of ammunition pretty quickly. Furthermore, if we knew there were civilians in a building we had no choice but to go in Green.

As we pushed through I thought that this was why I joined up: infantry skills being put into practice textbook fashion. Teddy and I were close to Corporal Parker as we went forward, jumping up on to the roofs to get eyes on as we went, each time checking the next compound in front for enemy, and engaging them with fire whenever we spotted them. The guys on the ground knew we were there giving them cover, which always gave them a boost, especially as they moved across open ground. The tactic was for the snipers to position themselves on the roofs, clear the way in front and give cover as the assaulting sections were blowing holes in walls, entering and clearing the buildings. As soon as they were clear, Teddy and I would jump down and head for the roof of a cleared building where we would then repeat the process. This was intense and knackering stuff, bearing in mind we were doing it in 40 degree heat with full body armour and equipment. I guess it was training and pure adrenaline that kept us moving at such a pace. I had started with four litres of water on me but by this time had already consumed half of that.

As we reached a point just short of the bridge, everything went very quiet and our advance slowed. 7 Platoon was now only about 200 metres from the bridge and halted in a graveyard. We could hear all the commanders talking over the radio net while they decided on the next move; as I had the radio I briefed Teddy on the situation. Shortly afterwards, 7 Platoon was ordered to advance to the bridge with 5 Platoon giving fire support from its position about 300 to 400 metres away.

We stood on a dusty track, with a treeline running from left to right in front of us with a small gap where track ran through. There were recently harvested poppies, so the crops were not too tall. We pushed through the tree line until we reached what I realised was a drainage ditch with a sort of mound of dirt to the left of us. As we went through I noticed that Private Thrumble had his oil bottle for his GPMG strapped to his helmet. I turned and said to Teddy, 'Looks like a Vietnam war film this.' He grinned and said, 'Yeah, it does.' As he spoke, we heard the whoosh of a RPG flying in towards us. It had been launched from the northern side of the bridge and passed between the last two guys from the section in front of us before detonating on the other side of the drainage ditch.

We threw ourselves down into the ditch as dust and debris flew all over the place and I heard the cracking of automatic fire as the Taliban opened up. Thankfully, the ditch was deep because the Taliban were firing like crazy, bullets literally whizzing and cracking all over the place and ricocheting off the ground in front of me. I just hugged the floor, flattening myself as close as I could to the ground. At that point, we could see two of our guys across from us lying motionless out in the open. Despite what was happening around us Teddy, who was an RMA 3 medic, leapt up shouting, 'They're hit! They're hit!' and started running full pelt towards them with bullets whistling around him and hitting the ground around his feet. I was shouting at him to keep low and stay down as I followed him, firing into the treeline on the other side.

I got down next to him when we reached the first guy, Gilly, who was lying there unconscious. As Teddy started to shake him, his eyes slowly flickered open as he regained consciousness. He began screaming and clutching at his knee, so we grabbed him and dragged him along with ourselves into the drainage ditch. He slid all the way down into the water, which was waist deep and, because the air temperature was so hot, absolutely freezing. He was still screaming in pain and clutching his knee, so we pulled his leg up to take a look and noticed a tear in his trousers and saw the blood. Teddy ripped the trouser leg open and saw a piece of shrapnel lodged just behind Gilly's kneecap. We asked if he could put any weight at all on it, but he was unable to do so.

In the meantime, the battle continued to rage around us. The noise was deafening, and foliage and twigs from the dense trees rained down on us. RPGs were literally criss-crossing over the top of our heads as we stood waist-deep in the water. I watched as two criss-crossed each other and smashed in to the ground on the other side of the ditch close to me. Lance Corporal Stevie Veal, who was second-in-command of Corporal Parker's section, came splashing along accounting for his men and saw that the other guy who had been knocked out had recovered consciousness. This left us with just Gilly and his shrapnel wound. In the army we have codes signifying a particular type of injury: a T1 casualty denotes someone totally unconscious but needing urgent hospital attention; T2 is anyone who cannot walk; T3 is walking wounded; and T4 is killed in action. So we told Stevie that we had a

T2 casualty and he said he would take him back. The platoon commander, Lieutenant Seal-Coon, appeared and reported the situation on his radio as Stevie hoisted Gilly up on his shoulders and started walking back. He looked at me and said, 'JC, take over my fire team.' I replied, 'No worries' while Teddy said that he would then go forward with Corporal Parker to help him out.

Lieutenant Seal-Coon went forward with Teddy to link up with Corporal Parker's section and get some fire down on the enemy, leaving me with Private Mclure and a few other guys under my command. Meanwhile, I could hear on the radio that 5 Platoon was now rushing over to our left flank to give us fire support. By this time, I had crawled up the eastern side of the drainage ditch from where I saw three Taliban running across another treeline some 300 metres away to our flank in an attempt to outflank us. I immediately took my safety catch off and fired at them, at the same time shouting, 'Enemy 300 metres, in treeline! Rapid fire, rapid fire!' My guys scrambled up the side of the ditch and opened fire on them. After around ten or fifteen minutes, Stevie came splashing back, completely exhausted and out of breath after evacuating Gilly and I briefed him on the situation before leaving him and pushing forward again to try to find Teddy.

I moved around a bend in the ditch, laughing to myself because, throughout all our training out on exercise, no matter where we were, be it the Brecon Beacons, Galloway Forest in Scotland, Salisbury Plain or wherever, we could guarantee we would end up wading through water. Never in a million years did I think that I would end wading through water waist-deep in the middle of a desert in Afghanistan under fire. At least they got something right in the training!

Reaching the end of the ditch, I found Lieutenant Seal-Coon with his map out, giving a full sitrep (situation report) over the radio. I kept flat as I emerged out of the ditch, crawling forward to ask about Teddy. Lieutenant Seal-Coon pointed over his shoulder to where I could see Teddy with his .338. Just as I reached him, he fired a round. A lifeless body fell out of a tree and Teddy, being half-American, whooped and yelled at the top of his voice, 'Yeah!' I tapped his right foot to let him know I was there. He turned. 'Did you see that? Did you see that!' To which I put my thumb up and said, 'Good shit man, you rock!'

I could see quite a thick, dense treeline to the left of the bridge near an old shack and started putting down fire into likely enemy positions while nearby Thrumble did the same with his GPMG, laying down excellent fire support. Josh Lee was also there, firing 40mm grenades from his SA80's UGL to the left and right of the bridge. Meanwhile Corporal Stu Parker was giving constant sitreps on the radio, reporting on everything including ammunition states. Watching him made me think that all those hours on training and exercise were being used to good effect, which is one of the reasons why the British Army is so professional.

I was observing the enemy who were only 60 or 70 metres away, when something caught my eye to the left of the small building. A head popped up and Teddy saw it – Bang! It was a head shot and a confirmed kill. Another Taliban swung around with his AK-47 on seeing his fellow fighter have his head blown off. Teddy moved his rifle across and once again – Bang! He looked at me with a slightly puzzled expression and said, 'What a twat!' He had clocked up three kills in the space of around five minutes.

Inspired by Teddy's performance, I was determined to find some targets of my own and began firing into likely enemy positions. Then out of nowhere three bullets whistled really close over my head. I glanced immediately through my SUSAT sight and observed a Taliban wrestling with his weapon, which had jammed. He sorted the problem out and, standing up, was aiming straight at me when I fired three rounds into him. He dropped straight down, a small plume of pink mist where each of my rounds hit him. Everything happened in slow motion. I grinned across at Teddy who had seen this happen and he gave me a thumbs-up.

At that point a bullet whizzed past literally centimetres from my face. I crawled back a bit and saw Private Thrumble putting a fresh belt of ammunition on his GPMG and yelled, 'Thrumble! Give me some covering fire!' He yelled back, 'Where?' I replied, 'Any f...ing where!' He grinned and slapped shut the top cover of his GPMG and then, with a wild stare in his eyes, just let fly, putting down heavy fire into the treeline to our left and allowing me to crawl out of there as fast as possible. I found Lieutenant Seal-Coon who was still there with his radio and maps, and reported that we were beginning to notch up some serious enemy kills. I asked him about the plan of action and whether we were going for the bridge. He relied, 'No, negative. We're pulling out.' He told me that we had achieved our objective and taken the fight to the enemy, and that the Vikings were now arriving to extract us. He ordered me to make my way back to Stevie Veal and double-check that he was ready to move. With that, I began splashing my way back through the drainage ditch.

Over the radio on my earpiece I suddenly heard, 'Man down!' On reaching Stevie I learned that it was Macca, the medic who had patched up Corporal Martin's arm. He had taken a round just below his body armour plate, right next to his belly button. He was a T1 casualty, but was fairly stable which was a relief.

I was telling Stevie about my first confirmed kill and Teddy's three kills when the Vikings appeared, their GPMGs laying down fire as they raced up towards us. Stevie's fire team had been ordered to move on. As they began to do so, I started to move forward and bumped into Lieutenant Seal-Coon who said, 'Where are you going, JC? We're mounting up and getting out!' I replied that I was not leaving without Teddy. Lieutenant Seal-Coon told me that Teddy was already with Corporal Parker and that he had just watched him get into his vehicle, so he was safe and well. With that I turned on my heels and jumped into the back of the Viking. It was chaos inside with everyone diving in as fast as possible because bullets were literally pinging off the sides of the vehicles. Within around thirty seconds they were moving again, stopping en route to pick up more guys en route during the withdrawal. We ended up at the medical point where we saw Macca lying doubled-up over on his side, being administered morphine and oxygen.

We were now on high ground and away from the contact, but the Vikings were moving back in and out of the area to ferry the other guys out. The Medical Officer told us that there was a Chinook helicopter coming in for Macca, so we all stripped off our kit, put our rifles and kit to one side, and manned the stretcher to get him aboard and away for proper medical treatment. The Chinook came in through the valley and over us, kicking up a massive amount of dust. As it landed, a protection team deployed and took up positions around the aircraft. The loadmaster came out and waved us forward, and we ran towards the paramedics standing at the end of the ramp. They took over and the protection team ran back on board, and within seconds the helicopter took off. From the time Macca had been shot to the point where he was in the hands of the medics at Camp Bastion was about thirty-five minutes so well within the 'Golden Hour' which is critical for the treatment of casualties.

At this point I still had not actually seen Teddy and was growing more than a little concerned as we walked back towards the Vikings. Shortly afterwards, I spotted him and along with everyone else we were soon rabbiting on about our experiences.

It was then time to mount up once again and move out to the middle of nowhere in the desert and set up camp. We cleaned our rifles, took on fresh ammunition and ate a decent amount of food. We then sat around the camp. If we had been in a non-tactical situation we would have lit a fire, but that of course would have been like someone shining a spotlight on us. So we sat in darkness checking radio batteries, cleaning weapons, loading up with new magazines, grenades and everything else we needed. Afterwards, we lay there with sleeping bags draped over us, because it was just too hot to climb into them, chatting and reflecting on what had happened that day. I remember feeling like a proper soldier now that I had been shot at for a sustained period and achieved my first confirmed kill. Teddy meanwhile kept the details of his kill to himself as he felt it was personal, between him and his target. It was a lot more of a ritual for him, one that he kept very much to himself.

We broke camp on the following morning and headed north and to the next village. I'm not sure whether it was a relief or an anti-climax, but the next few villages proved largely unoccupied, almost like ghost towns as we went through and cleared them. The plan was to continue driving the Taliban northwards towards Musa Qaleh, which was the last major city where there was still a degree of Taliban control existing. There was no intention of us going into battle there, as we did not have sufficient manpower, so the objective was to ensure we cleared the Taliban along the Helmand River and continued pushing them north. At this point, it was early May and the heat was stifling with temperature of 40 degrees during the day, dropping to around 20 degrees at night.

Initially we were to stop off at FOB Robinson and carry out patrols around Sangin itself, which was where A Company was now located. As mentioned previously, the area around the FOB was heavily mined. The inevitable happened as we drove across country towards the FOB when one of the vehicles towards the front went over a mine. Fortunately no one was killed but there were a few casualties. One of them was Sergeant Keith Nieves, along with a Fijian lad called Private Nadriva, who pulled Sergeant Nieves out the vehicle, and the Marine driver. Whereas Teddy and I were travelling together, Deano and Scotty were with this convoy but in separate vehicles. It was Scotty's misfortune to be in that particular Viking; although he was unharmed, he had strapped his sniper rifle to the roof of the vehicle which burst into flames. Forced to abandon his kit, he walked away with nothing apart from his pistol. His laser rangefinder and the rest of his sniper kit was now gone, leaving him 'combat ineffective.' In the event, he was fortunate in that he was due his mid-tour R & R break in eight days, so he was flown to Camp Bastion where he was employed helping B Company's headquarters to forward mail and kit to us on ops before being flown back to the UK.

This led to some reorganisation. Our section commander, Deano, and Teddy, a shooter, had to be the obvious pairing, leaving me with two real options. I could either carry on with them, so we would have two spotters and a shooter, or I could backfill into B Company temporarily for the three weeks that Scotty would be away and then depart on R & R. In the end we all agreed that it would actually be easier if we kept to the normal two-man operation.

I slotted into 5 Platoon, whose platoon sergeant was Sergeant Chris Caneper, the guy whom I met in the Snake Pit at FOB Robinson when we first arrived. He was from the Gibraltar Regiment and had volunteered for the tour, replacing Sergeant Nieves. The platoon's 51mm mortar man was Private Nadriva – the very same who had nearly blown up Teddy and me during training at Camp Bastion at the beginning of the tour. Nadriva had been wounded and so I was to replace him. I was really chuffed about this because I would get my hands on a different weapon system, my role being to provide support for the platoon by firing high explosive, smoke and illumination bombs.

We camped in FOB Robinson, unfortunately not in the nice cushy buildings that we had occupied previously as these were being occupied by 2 RTR which was now based there. We were to live in the Dust Bowl and there was a good reason for it being dubbed that – it was very, very dusty. The stuff actually came up to our ankles and, with the consistency of flour, it penetrated everywhere. If someone walked through it, you would see this massive trail of dust kicked up everywhere. It was a nightmare at the best of times, but we had no option but to live with it. The best answer was to take a large bottle of water, move away from the vehicles and then tip it all over our heads and wash our hair and faces or otherwise we just looked like ghosts. We had to do this because our mouths and nostrils were parched and our tonsils on fire because they had been so dried out by the dust. Along with fighting a continual battle to keep ourselves clean, our number one priority was to make sure that our rifles were always spotless and lightly oiled. The chance of anyone attacking a fortified army camp was unlikely, but we had to at least be ready just in case. That said, we eventually took to leaving our weapons in the vehicles, the only alternative being literally to clean them every half an hour.

On the first morning in the Dust Bowl, Pete Tointon came down looking for Teddy, Deano and me. He had gone to talk with the Canadians and had succeeded in coming away with some their rations which were not dissimilar to those of the Americans. That day, I enjoyed the best boil-in-the bag meal I have ever tasted and probably ever will – it was veal steak in a mushroom sauce and they had not skimped on the steak, with beautiful large chunks. I can still recall it now, a taste sensation.

We had been in the FOB for about two days when the call came in for us to move out as we were going to be moving into Sangin. Due to its large size, it was decided to break the convoy down into two main elements. The leading element would leave around mid-afternoon and the second an hour or so later.

As I was about to move out in my new role as the mortar man, I was going through last-minute reminders because I had not touched the 51mm mortar since my 9 Platoon days some three years previously. An indirect fire weapon, effective use of it is about finding the correct angles for different ranges. Sergeant Caneper and Corporal Thorn went over and over the drills with me until I could do them all without any prompting.

I had to repack my day sack because in place of my laser rangefinder and other tools of the sniper's trade, I would be carrying mortar bombs. The guys in the platoon would also be carrying extra bombs for me to help with the load as they weigh quite a bit. I was carrying five HE and three smoke bombs as well as my rifle ammunition, water and all the rest of my equipment, which would make up a total load of 70 to 80 pounds.

The lead element of the convoy mounted up and headed off. During the following hour, we all sat waiting and after a while saw a large plume of black smoke rising up from Sangin in the distance. We all joked that the locals were probably having a massive barbecue while at the same time praying that nothing had gone amiss. Sure enough, ten or fifteen minutes later the lead element's Viking vehicles came scrambling up the road towards us and through the front gate of FOB Robinson. There were in a bad way with bullet holes in them, bits of bar armour hanging off and smashed windows.

They had been ambushed just inside Sangin, near an area that was sort of a local reference point or landmark that people called the 'Chinese tea shop' or something similar. When the guys arrived, one of them had sworn blind that he had seen a child come close with a mobile phone doing what we called 'dicking', a term coined in Northern Ireland which meant reporting on the movement of troops and their whereabouts.

As the convoy came up the road Deano was on top cover, standing up in a hatch in the roof of the Viking vehicle in which he and Teddy were travelling. Just behind him, strapped to the roof, were jerrycans of fuel and other items of kit. At that point a Taliban fighter launched an RPG from a nearby rooftop and scored a direct hit on the roof of the vehicle, detonating on one of the jerrycans and causing a huge fireball that totally engulfed Deano in burning fuel. He dropped down back through the hatch of the vehicle, desperately trying to put out the flames and ripping off his helmet and body armour. Teddy meanwhile placed his hand on the handle of the rear door, readying himself to open it, but could hear the sound of rounds pinging off the armour the outside. The Taliban had learned where our doors were and created a choice for those inside: either stay inside and burn to death or open the doors and get riddled with bullets.

At this point Deano jumped back up into the hatch of the vehicle, with no helmet or any body armour, and began to return fire with his SA80 rifle. At the same time, there was a lull of a few moments in the bullets hitting the rear door, so Teddy threw it open and, armed only with his 9mm pistol, leapt out and headed for a nearby an alleyway. There was deafening noise and dust all around him as bullets rained down and RPGs flew in all from all directions. As he scrambled into the alleyway, he came face to face with a Taliban fighter shooting rounds in to the air and screaming, '*Allahu akbar*!' Teddy shot him dead on the spot before turning his attention back to the Viking. Realising that there was no movement from it, he ran back to the vehicle where he found Deano lying unconscious inside, having been knocked out by the blast of another RPG hitting the roof.

Deano was in a mess. Severely burned from the blast and injured by shrapnel, he was losing blood and rapidly losing consciousness. He needed emergency medical treatment and quickly as he was in a really bad way. Teddy got into the vehicle and dragged him out of the vehicle, all the while under fire from RPGs and automatic weapons. He then had to carry him whilst continuously getting shot at with machine gun fire. Somehow, he succeeded in reaching another Viking, throwing open the doors and heaving Deano inside. There was no room for him so he had no choice but to run back another 50 or 60 metres, still under heavy fire, to another vehicle where he took cover in the back of it

All the while the FSTs were bringing fire down on the enemy, but there were buildings all around and it was a relatively built-up town, with high buildings all around that area which made manoeuvring almost impossible. The convoy was still under very heavy fire as it drove out of Sangin. As soon as it reached a safe area on the way back to FOB Robinson, a Chinook arrived to collect Deano and the other casualties who were flown to Camp Bastion. Deano made it there within twenty-five or thirty minutes, again well within the Golden Hour, which we all still believe saved his life. Apparently four different surgeons worked on him all through the night in order to stabilise him initially and then keep him alive. It took a lot of work to bring him back.

When I heard what had happened my first concern was for Deano, but I also worried about Teddy. The guy had done us all proud. I found out that he was at the medical station where he was being treated for shock rather than wounds. Both can be equally serious though and I do not want to underplay the physiological effects of war, especially when you realise what Teddy had taken on and beaten.

I bumped into Hughesy, who was part of the FST team, holding a first field dressing to his face as I asked what had happened to him. He pulled it away and there was a graze the same width as a 7.62mm bullet right across his cheek. On contact, they had leapt out of the vehicle as it had all kicked off, but his day sack had been caught on the door. As he leaned down to free it, he had felt a violent blow to his face which knocked him flat. He instinctively curled up expecting another blow. It turned out that a bullet had come very near to taking his head off, close enough to take layers of skin from his face. He just sat there, saying really slowly, 'Yeah, I know, I know.' All of the guys were in varying degrees of shock, no matter how they dealt with it and all had what I can only describe as the 'thousand yard stare.' Being in and around the guys that had come back from the ambush reminded me of watching a television documentary about soldiers from the past or even seeing old photographs of soldiers from the Seconnd World

War, only here it was in full colour and with modern kit, but they had the same look in their eyes. We subsequently heard that a couple of Apache helicopters were swiftly deployed over Sangin and destroyed some of the Taliban fleeing the scene on mopeds.

While I was listening to everyone's versions of events amid what seemed to be endless chain smoking, Teddy appeared from the medical area. He was really very quiet and staring at the floor as I went over and put my arm round him, saying, 'Nice one mate, you did brilliantly from what I've heard.' He was almost lost for words and just kept saying, 'Hope he makes it, hope he makes it.' I replied, 'Me too buddy.'

After my prompting him for a while, he told me what had happened but even then would stop and stare into space as if he was re-living the experience or replaying things in his head. I put this down to the shock. As the next few hours went by, he distanced himself from the group and wanted to be left alone, so Colour Sergeant Snow asked me to keep an eye on him and report anything I thought was not great. Of course I would have done this anyway, because he was my oppo and I was going to look out for him. In addition, with Deano now injured, that now made me section commander.

Teddy and I now had no kit at all, absolutely nothing. Much had been destroyed, not only by the Taliban but also by the Apaches which had ensured that the Taliban did not benefit from the situation. I was left with the clothes I stood up in; for the next few days, I even had to clean my teeth by eating about three packs of chewing gum each morning. We managed to get a bit of a whip round going and obtained a few items. The whole unit had not been back to Camp Bastion for quite some time so nothing was washed and, no matter how desperate, I was not going to start wearing other men's sweaty boxer shorts.

On the weapons front, Teddy managed to acquire an L96 which was a sharpshooter's rifle and had a different scope to ours. It was not much use to us because all our shooting data was for the .338 as opposed to a 7.62mm calibre weapon. This rendered me useless because my role was to spot everything and give ranges. Teddy, on the other hand, was a qualified sniper and more than capable of using this weapon so he joined Corporal Parker's section in B Company.

I meanwhile continued as the 51mm mortar man within my group. This meant that we lived in the Dust Bowl for another four days, sleeping by the vehicles and going through the same mundane daily routine. People were even putting up ponchos and making little walls out of anything available. That said, the camaraderie was just excellent but we were still bored, so I was sent on a mission to try and acquire some American MREs (Meals, Ready to Eat) which I am relieved to say was successful. Teddy was also bored and went across to the shooting range on the northern side of the FOB, an area next to a mound near the wall on which you could stand and fire over it into a big area of basically nothing. We would pick out prominent rocks and there was even an ISO container which you could target and just practise our marksmanship. We simply told the boss that we were off to the range to check zero and we would just practise and fire off rounds. The ammunition on the .338 rifle was in really low supply, but there was no shortage of 7.62mm or 5.56mm so we spent hours up there shooting off rounds, talking and sharing a smoke.

A few guys came to test their GPMGs and even some Americans came over with an M4 carbine on a bi-pod, so we swapped and they had a go on the L96 while we did likewise with their weapon. I remember one of the Americans asking, 'You're a sniper?' As I nodded, Teddy zapped a road with the laser rangefinder and measured that it was exactly a kilometre away. The American said, 'Betcha can't hit that road, man.' We realised that he wanted us to land a round on the track 1,000 metres away. Also, we only had an old scope but we accepted the challenge anyway.

Both Teddy and I held our breath and a few seconds later were whooping and doing high fives, because we both did it first time. The American smiled broadly, shook his head and said we British snipers were crazy. It was nice to have the praise that all the American guys gave us and we ended up going over to their area to play American Touch Football, which was really amusing because we were still in the Dust Bowl. With all the dust thrown up, it was total chaos because we could not see anything and at times might as well have been running around chasing a ball blindfolded. The amount of times people would blindly run into each other was countless. We did this kind of thing for the next four days and I read the same magazines over and over again. I also used the opportunity to send letters home to Annie while receiving some very welcome mail. It was really good to hear from back home.

Eventually we received the call that we were to move out and into Sangin, so we began to prepare ourselves and pack things up. We also heard that Ross Kemp was on his way out to us and would be appearing soon with his film crew. He arrived at the FOB, which broke the monotony, and I remember meeting him, saying hello and shaking his hand. It was quite late at night when he turned up, so we all got our heads down shortly afterwards.

CHAPTER 10

Sangin

We moved into Sangin from FOB Robinson for our next deployment, Operation LASTAY KULANG. Our arrival was uneventful, the streets being busy as we drove past the vehicle from which Teddy had rescued Deano, now just an empty burnt-out shell. Having settled in, we took advantage of the nearby river. At this point, we had been away from Camp Bastion for a number of weeks and, having been unable to shower at all, were understandably keen to get into the water and wash ourselves properly. The current was very strong and you had to be careful to avoid being dragged downstream. The water was icy, its temperature bliss after the scorching heat of the day.

We remained in this area for the day and then began preparing to move out on patrols. We headed towards the northwest, approaching a wadi which led to Musa Qalah, the last major town the Taliban held in our region. We were under orders not to touch it. Previously, the Paras had gone in there, cleared the town and held it before leaving after the signing of a secret truce in late 2006 under which British forces withdrew in return for the Taliban not attacking the region. At the beginning of February 2007, a force of up to 200 Taliban attacked and captured the town, imprisoning all the tribal chiefs who had agreed to the truce.

We moved around the perimeter of Sangin and some of the built-up areas which were quiet. One minute you would be moving through a treeline or open countryside and the next be surrounded by houses, compounds and alleyways. We would arrive in a new area and sometimes be surrounded by people all staring at us. The majority of the time they were hostile and stared at us intimidatingly, but we could not allow that to happen and simply stood our ground and stared straight back. If they smiled and waved then we would of course reciprocate because winning hearts and minds was essential. We continued patrolling through the markets and then back into the alleyways where kids would be playing, running around screaming and yelling, before we emerged once again into the surrounding fields. Meanwhile, we were well aware that we were being watched closely and followed all the time.

At one point, we rounded a corner and saw a young boy a little way off, sitting on his own with his knees drawn up to his chest, hugging his legs. As I drew level with him, I glanced at his face and saw that it was totally devoid of expression. I then observed the needle laying near him and recalled the serious problem of heroin addiction in the region. I put a small bottle of water on the ground next to him and carried on.

We were out of the main area now and continued past loads of smashed up buildings with no one around at all and by this time had gone for around a kilometre without seeing a soul. In the distance I saw Sangin DC coming into view and realised that this was the area that I had seen on YouTube where the Paras had gone in with all guns blazing and firing from rooftops. This meant that it was only a year previously that the Taliban had been stood here fighting our boys as they came in. I imagined the firepower and the bombs that would have come in, realising that anyone in these buildings would have stood no chance at all. We saw the bombs go in on film, but then the cameras stopped and we did not see the after effects.

On the following day we were called to a briefing, following which we all stood behind the main building housing the headquarters element where there is a courtyard with a memorial listing the names of the guys that had died in that area. There had been a Dane who had died recently, so we gathered around the memorial to pay our respects to him. Immediately after this, a large amount of mail arrived.

The next day, we left at 3.00 am and patrolled for around four or five hours, mostly under the cover of darkness. Instead of moving north into the middle of nowhere, we headed south and into the built-up areas of Sangin that were largely deserted at that hour. We arrived at a sort of over-pass that ran above a canal where, as the sun rose, we packed away our night vision scopes. It was fascinating to watch the city come alive as the sun came up, in front of our eyes, the voices of the mullahs echoing from the tops of mosques as they called the faithful to prayer.

We continued to patrol through a maze of streets and alleyways, sometimes with roofs over us and sometimes finding ourselves in wide open spaces as if the city had simply disappeared. We walked past an alleyway where there were some really deep scratches or grooves in the wall running away from us, and it became obvious that these had been made by small arms fire during what had clearly been a pretty intense firefight.

As we moved back through to the market area, with everyone still staring at us, a minibus screeched around a corner and sped directly towards us. Sergeant Chris Caneper decided he did not the look of it and, raising his rifle, fired a round in front of the vehicle, the bullet ricocheting up and smashing the windscreen. The driver leaped out of the vehicle with his hands up, shouting, 'No, Mr! No, Mr! No Taliban! No Taliban.' Chris shouted back, 'Slow down!' We continued the patrol, returning to our base at around 7.00 am.

On one occasion, we went across to a location on the outskirts of Sangin called Patrol Base Waterloo, which was occupied by an operational mentoring liaison team (OMLT) whose role was to train ANA units to secure areas and fight the Taliban. On the way, again quite early in the morning, we stopped in an alleyway and I checked a doorway to my right which led towards a door to a compound. I knelt down next to this doorway and lit a cigarette; as I did so, I heard a rustling coming from behind me. Dropping the cigarette, I spun around with my rifle to my shoulder, safety catch off, and saw a little old man who looked a bit like Gandhi, but wearing a turban, sitting there looking at me.

We remained in this alleyway for a while, waiting for the rest of the patrol to meet us from the other direction and move into position, but they were delayed by the horde of kids that was surrounding them and asking for sweets or water. I remained in the alley and once again heard some rustling from the same direction, so I slowly moved my head around the doorway again to see the old man walking towards me, saying something in either Pashto or Dari. I put my hand up to tell him to stop, but he kept walking, pointing to his chest and then pointing to the alleyway and repeating this gesture. I put my hand up again and asked him in slow deliberate English, 'You want to come out here?' I pointed to the alleyway, receiving enthusiastic nods of agreement. I told the guys that a civilian was coming through and waved the old man through as he put his hand up to thank me and disappeared on his way.

By this time the others had got themselves in to position, so we continued on our way to Patrol Base Waterloo. When we arrived, we could hear the sound of mopeds, something we had registered earlier during the patrol. It appeared that two Afghans had been following us, appearing at the end of alleyways and then vanishing, only to reappear a few minutes later. We were clearly being followed, but we had not spotted any weapons or observed the use of any mobile phones. We knew though that it was more than likely that they were working for the Taliban, counting us and seeing which direction we were heading. There was not a great deal we could do, because we could not see any weapons or actual evidence of a direct threat, so I guess the only thing we could have done was to pursue them and arrest them. In any case, they were on mopeds while we were on our flat feet with over 60 pounds on our backs. We entered the patrol base over whose walls we could clearly observe the two guys on mopeds sitting out in the open watching us. We let off a few warning shots off in their direction and they disappeared.

After that we began patrolling from the base, our task being to draw the Taliban out for a fight, As we patrolled down a steep hill through the Green Zone, amongst the fields and towards the low ground on the edge of Sangin, we had ANA behind us. Eventually, we reached an area with around four or five buildings. We were approaching the left hand side of one of them when I suddenly heard one of our guys screaming, 'Get down! Get down!' I instantly crouched low as I looked in his direction. It turned out that he had seen in the corner of his eye a boy of around fifteen years old with something in his hand, so he had automatically spun round with his rifle pointing towards the youngster's face. Terrified, the lad had dropped the radio he had been holding and was holding his hands in the air. Our guy apologised to us, saying that he thought the boy was a suicide bomber with a detonator in his hand.

We carried on patrolling towards the buildings, but as we did so we all heard a loud crack as someone fired a round at us, followed by more. I instantly looked for cover, sprinting forward towards the end of the building where I saw a few of our guys dart around the corner. I took cover and listened to the sporadic firing, unable to see where it was originating. I looked around and saw our guys moving in trying to find where the fire was coming from, while others were putting down covering fire with GPMGs. There was a large metal door behind us, which creaked open. The lad next to me and I spun around, weapons raised, and saw a woman covered from head to toe in black, with just her eyes showing. Despite our being unable to understand a word she was saying, we realised she was attempting to shoo us away. I was pretty pumped up with adrenaline after being shot at and wanted her to just get back inside to safety, but she wasn't listening and continued to gesture towards us. We had to be really careful not to overstep the mark and had been briefed to tread carefully, because in Afghan culture it is easy to offend by even making eye contact with a woman without permission. I clearly could not physically move her back into safety, so tried to intimidate her by moving forward stamping my feet loudly as I did so, but she wasn't having any of it and continued her stream of verbal abuse. I could see there were children and another woman inside the door, so in the end I took another step forward and shouted, 'Get inside and lock the door!' With this, she finally got the message and rushed inside and I heard the door being bolted.

By this time the firing had completely stopped, so we pushed forward to a small stream where Sergeant Caneper positioned me to the left of a bridge. I unpacked the 51mm mortar and a few HE bombs while the guys in 5 Platoon spread themselves out along the stream area. We then called in fire support and I dropped some bombs into the area where we expected the Taliban to be but with no result. Absolutely nothing happened, so we moved back along the stream and through the fields towards a dried-up river bed which was under the cover of trees which provided welcome shade from the heat. We continued along this route under the trees for quite some time until all of a sudden we took a left turn and headed up a very steep hill. We had been patrolling in the heat for several hours and the hill was sandy and rocky, proving to be a nightmare to climb. Our kit was bloody heavy and we would get up about four paces before losing our footing and slipping backwards. My legs were burning and I could hear ringing in my ears.

We eventually made it to the top where we found the WMIKs providing over-watch and ready to give covering fire as we made the ascent. From there, we made our way back into Sangin DC where we were told to clean our weapons and do our post-patrol admin before getting our heads down for a bit. I did this and then stripped down to just my trousers, before stepping into my Viking vehicle and grabbing a copy of *Maxim*. As I sat down and relaxed, I heard a single gunshot and thought, 'Oh, for f...'s sake!' As an NCO, when a negligent discharge happened, I would have to charge whoever the offender was. As I got out of the vehicle I saw a stretcher being whisked past by four Marines and a medic. It was Lance Corporal George Davey who subsequently died of his injuries, leaving a wife and two daughters. In due course the inquest determined that, 'He died in a tragic firearms incident.' He was a really good guy and was in fact a Christian man who, although not being the hard-core bible thumping type, had a real belief in God. It was so tragic and affected morale, leaving all of our spirits really low.

Along with this, Corporal Darren Bonner had been killed after his Viking had been hit by a mine and these two instances had happened within eight days of each other. It was around this time that I remember calling, texting and writing to Annie quite a lot, but although we had all hoped we would be moving back to camp Bastion, we received orders that we were to be moving out to the north of Sangin. We had not been back to Bastion for six weeks and had totally forgotten what air conditioning felt like, that's for sure.

I had at least managed to acquire a sleeping bag and had the toothbrush and toothpaste my family had sent out, but was still waiting for replacement socks and underwear for which I was desperate. It makes me laugh now to think of my limited kit, which had been lent to me or sent from my family, strapped to the Viking vehicle in a black bin bag, wedged between two bergens to stop it flapping around.

So this was life in Sangin – going out on patrol, making sure we were nice to the locals and coming in again. Eventually, we received notice that we had one last patrol to complete before we moved on to our next deployment and were to have all our kit packed away ready to move out after the patrol.

We patrolled out towards the south, through Sangin and the maze of alleyways, fields, dried-up riverbeds and markets. Right at the end of the patrol, we skirted out and around past Deano's vehicle once more. I looked at it, recalling how I had strapped my bergen to it and realising that the Taliban had picked their ambush spot well with the built-up area providing no real room for the vehicles to manoeuvre out of it. In fact, how we got out is beyond me, but somehow we escaped with a few casualties but no deaths. Shortly afterwards, the Vikings arrived and we all jumped in before heading back to the DC. Later, we drove out into the middle of nowhere ready to receive our orders for Operation LASTAY KULANG.

CHAPTER 11

Operation
LASTAY KULANG

This was the last part of our deployment on MOGs and we had so far succeeded in pushing the Taliban from the south, northwards up through the middle of Sangin, and now were to clear much of the Green Zone to the north of Sangin, still close to the Helmand river. The plan was that once we had cleared the Taliban from this area, we would build another forward operating base here, to be called FOB Inkerman. This was going to be another big operation, so A Company, based in Sangin, came out to support us, deploying further to the north and executing a kind of pincer movement. We were to cross the 611 road which was the main supply route that ran all the way from Kajaki in the north, hugging the Helmand River down past Sangin. It finally joins the A1, which equates to the M25 but encircling the entire country rather than just a city.

Essentially, the plan was to stop the Taliban from moving into the north of Sangin by inserting a forward operating base there, having cleared the area first. Just opposite this area was a large wadi which in size was more like a dried-up valley that swept right up to Musa Qalah, providing the Taliban with an escape route from Sangin. It would not be our task to chase them through to Musa Qalah and take fresh ground, but to push them back and away from our positions and the territory we were to take and hold.

We spent that first night underneath the stars, cleaning our weapons, preparing them and ourselves ready for battle. Everyone deals with these kinds of circumstances in their own way, I loaded up the Arctic Monkeys on to my iPod and put on my headphones, lying there listening to the music and thankfully managing to get quite a bit of sleep.

Major Mick Aston had decided that he wanted a full sniper asset again, so Teddy and I were reunited to work as a team again. He still only had the L96 rifle, which he had acquired from the sharpshooters, while all I had was my laser rangefinder and my CWS for my SA80 rifle. We also had our PRR to communicate with each other while I was equipped with a Bowman radio, which provided communications with every other commander on the ground. I carried six litres of water in addition to a pistol in a holster strapped to my leg, and four magazines strapped to my other leg in a double leg pouch with another two in my pouches on my Osprey body armour. We were running around in extreme heat carrying approximately 70 pounds of kit. As Teddy was the designated shooter, I wanted to try to reduce his load so that his heart rate would stay down, enabling him to engage targets properly. I carried much of his ammunition and other items as well as all my own front line scales, so my kit was really heavy. I treated myself to two packs of Super Noodles this time and squirted two Yorkie bars into my mouth to make sure my energy levels were as high as possible, ready for the next day.

We woke up quite early, just as the sun was coming up, and drove to some high ground overlooking the Green Zone. We parked the Vikings some distance away and dismounted to spread out and carry out final radio checks. We were attached to 7 Platoon again, moving with Corporal Parker's section, but Deano and Scotty were not around and Major Aston had told me that he wanted major sniper cover for the company. We were well aware that we were going to be covering a lot more ground than usual.

We pushed forward towards the Green Zone and could see it stretching out in front of us as we came down from the high ground, making our way past some compounds that looked as though they had not been occupied for a while. There was a deathly hush with no activity or people out and about, the normal calm before the storm as the locals clearly knew something was going to happen. It was only too obvious that we were about to be involved in a heavy contact.

We reached the road where we took cover in one of the deep drainage ditches that lined it on either side, staying for a while and watching the road while discussing the next move. We decided that we would move across to the road and push in properly. After crossing the road we began moving forward, and I remember it just being so deathly quiet. We came across another compound and at that point came under fire, the cracks from the bullets resounding around us as we kicked in the door of the compound, quickly double checking it was empty as we took cover. There were three rooms towards the end of the compound and we discovered the third room on the right had been painted totally black by soot. This, together with a few holes in the walls, provided us with the perfect position for a sniper so I called up Teddy on my PRR. He came running in and took up his position while I found an old blanket covered in crap and straw and hung this up behind him to ensure no silhouette of him could be seen, so we were now in a position where if anyone looked in, they would see nothing, just total pitch darkness.

One of our Minimi LMG gunners was just outside, so I pulled him into the room we were in because it was the perfect place from which to give covering fire for the guys coming up. It was now time for us to move, so I grabbed Teddy and we followed Corporal Parker's section across to the drainage ditch. It was quite high, around chest height, with shallow water underfoot, so we were running along bent down, zig zagging along the ditch. We stopped short and braced ourselves while the guys blew a mousehole in one of the compounds to provide entry to it; as they did so we were observing for any sign of the enemy, ready to give cover. There were a few compounds in the distance covered with trees and the crops in places were quite high, so it was difficult to see because we were quite low down in the ditch.

There was a loud bang to our right as the guys punched another mousehole in the wall. I grabbed Teddy's shoulder and indicated that we were going to push up to where they were going in. We got the call on the PRR, 'Compound clear, compound clear,' so moved straight

Camouflage and concealment training in Brecon 2006.

Getting into a fire position during a stalk in Brecon 2006.

Making use of the lay back position in Brecon 2006.

Author observing the landscape during an observation exercise Brecon 2006.

A WMIK (Weapons Mount Installation Kit) Landrover. Fitted with a GPMG (General Purpose Machine Gun) and a .50 Cal machine gun.

Me on patrol in Sangin.

A Javelin missile being launched.

Me with a L115 (.338) sniper rifle on a rooftop in Nowzad. A sangar from the DC is visible behind me.

B Company lads taking a break in the Green zone.

Re-supply by Chinook.

Me and Teddy on a roof top in Joucelay during Op Lastay Kulang.

Teddy in Kajaki with Charlie, one of our adopted dogs.

Kajaki Sofla from OP Sparrow-Hawk. It clearly shows the different terrain of mountains, flats, and Green zone.

Getting some air support in Kajaki Sofla.

The reservoir in Kajaki.

Me and Teddy after a patrol in Kajaki. I am carrying an L96 and Teddy has an L115.

A soldier from Recce Platoon on patrol in Nowzad, part of our Quick reaction force during Sniper Ops.

Aviators and beards. Snipers from left to right TM, OB, JL and Kingy.

up, crawling over the rubble in front of the hole. Inside, the compound was ideal for us because there were stairs leading to the roof, with three rooms in a similar layout to the previous house in which we had taken cover. We got ourselves up on the roof, which was flat and had a sort of foot-high parapet enabling us crawl along it without exposing ourselves as targets. There was a hole in the parapet, so I called down to one of the engineers for a hooligan tool, a heavy crowbar-type tool.

I began to hack away at the hole to make it a bit bigger, while taking my day sack off for Teddy to use as a support, in order for him to be able to aim through the hole without having the barrel sticking out of it. Teddy positioned himself around half a metre back from it while I moved down to another aperture and, using my laser rangefinders, zapped the tree line nearby and gave the range to Teddy. I continued this process, giving distances and ranges for the whole area and terrain in around us. I would always try to provide information on prominent land marks staggered outwards, so one would be about 100 metres away, followed by another 200 metres away and continue outwards, creating almost a virtual distance range out of the landscape and things within it. This way Teddy could change the range on his dial swiftly and score a direct hit. We stayed up there for quite a while because we had been told to remain where we were, as we were now conveniently central to 7 Platoon while the other platoons were also moving up.

We then spotted some enemy moving from the left to our right, so I reported to the OC on the radio and described what we were watching. They were withdrawing, but not along the river, moving instead up the Green Zone some 500 metres away. They knew exactly where we were and were making sure they were not anywhere near us. While this was going on, I suddenly noticed the left-hand side of my body was getting somewhat sweaty and felt a tingling sensation on my thigh. Rolling over, I noticed black smoke and realised that the room below was on fire. I crawled away from the area and fortunately at that point we were told to move out.

Teddy and I attached ourselves to Corporal Mason's section of 5 Platoon, moving along the drainage ditch next to the 611 road where we came under fire from an enemy sniper. We were told to locate him urgently. I came across Major Aston as we moved on, and explained that there was only Teddy and me, and that a sniper-on-sniper scenario quite often took a long time to resolve. He understood and told us that he was not looking for miracles and to try our best to locate the sniper.

We eventually came to a point where another road forked off from the 611 road, leading up towards the Taliban. This meant that we had to scramble up and out of the drainage ditch, run across a road into the open and back down into the drainage ditch, so the call went out for one of our guys to lay down some really heavy covering fire us as we crossed over. As we ran across the road, we both heard a single loud crack. The enemy sniper had obviously seen us and opened fire, his round passing between us. Teddy now fancied his chances, because we now had a good idea of the opponent's approximate location – there was only one building in the near vicinity, surrounded by fields with crops. The sniper clearly could not be in the crops because they would have obscured his vision, so common sense dictated that he was somewhere in the building.

We moved up and, as our guys began to move in to clear the compound, Teddy and I both had our scopes trained on the building. Suddenly, I spotted a figure in white with a black turban and followed him as he came around the corner of the building about 200 metres away, holding an AK-47. I watched as he fired towards some of our guys to my left, before lining him up and firing a few rounds from my SA80. I watched him drop and chalked up another confirmed kill. There was then another crack of a round as it clipped a tree behind me just above my head before ricocheting into the branches of another just behind that. The enemy sniper was still out there but had clearly changed his position, something we needed to do as well and pretty damn quick.

With the compound now clear, we moved in and looked to see how we could position ourselves up on the roof, but in this case we needed one of the lads to bring a ladder for us. Once on the roof, we did not have a great deal of joy in spotting the enemy's movements due to the proximity of the treeline, so we stayed up there while our troops moved around and onwards.

We were essentially chasing the Taliban in parallel fashion – they were in the Green Zone moving northeast, while we were just on the edge of the zone, opposite to the 611, also pushing north east. It was a sort of race, as we crossed another road and zig zagged along, jumping back down in the drainage ditch. We approached up one road, which swept away from the 611 and led all the way to a few compounds spread out diagonally to each other with large trees between them. The plan was for us to push along this road and get ourselves into these buildings and then into the Green Zone itself. We moved down this road at quite a pace, heading towards the compounds as quickly as possible, the boys kicking the doors. In a few minutes we heard the shouts of, 'Compound clear, compound clear!'

Once again, Teddy and I made our way on to a roof, followed closely by the FAC who had a couple of Dutch Apache helicopters on standby overhead. We also had the MFC who was getting ready to bring some mortar fire in as well. The enemy fire had died down a bit at this point, as we had a couple of GPMG guys laying down fire. One of them was a Grenadier Guardsman from Manchester called Tommo, who had volunteered to come on tour with us. He and another guy were laying down fire with their GPMGs towards a compound that was around 300 to 400 metres away to our half-right, as we had been taking fire from there.

Teddy moved himself along the wall and was now facing directly into the Green Zone and I moved myself up to where the GPMG guys were, because I could see Tommo was having trouble with a stoppage, and got on my hands and knees and helped him clear it. I remember noticing that the other guy was just watching us, so I said, 'What's wrong – can't you see anyone?' By this time Tommo had sorted himself out and said, 'I see them, I see them' and began to lay fire down again. I turned to the other guy and said, 'Look mate, just watch Tommo's tracer. Not continual fire, just keep it slow in bursts because you don't want to waste ammo.' Between them, they put down a nice steady rate of fire into the building, switching it from doors to windows and around the place.

As I turned round, I saw Ross Kemp and his camera crew. To this day, it was a proud moment for my arse to be on national television. I said, 'All right, Ross?' He replied, 'Yep. All okay with you, mate?' Major Aston then gave him a briefing as to what was happening, and I sat down next to Stewart, the FAC, who was busy talking to the two Dutch Apache attack helicopters circling overhead, and looked over in the same direction as Teddy and Josh Lee. The two GPMG guys got down from the roof as their section was to move on to another tasking, while Corporal Parkinson's section moved into the compound with Woody to take up position there for a while. Teddy spotted some movement by the Taliban a few hundred metres away through a hole in a wall about 6 feet high, which ran from left to right. The hole was where it looked like a high explosive had taken a chunk out of the wall and Teddy had seen Taliban running from one side to the other. He pointed it out to Josh, who had a UGL attached to his SA80 rifle, and readied himself to fire. Josh aimed his launcher and fired, and we watched the grenade detonate; if anyone was anywhere near that hole they were either dead or, at the very least, in a world of hurt.

Out of nowhere at that moment, the enemy fired an RPG straight at us and I watched Ross Kemp duck down shouting, 'F...ing hell!' Meanwhile beside me, Stewart was going crazy with the Dutch Apache helicopters because they had not yet identified where we were and therefore could not fire. Stewart asked me to pop one of my signal smoke grenades and throw it over the wall, so I did and we watched the plume of orange smoke drift upwards. As it happened, the Apaches still couldn't identify the smoke. By this time Stewart was going absolutely mental, saying: 'If you cannot identify bright orange smoke, how are you going to fire on the right target!' I threw another one, this time purple, and the helicopters finally spotted it.

While this was going on, Teddy had been quietly looking through his scope trying to locate the RPG gunner who had fired on us; out of nowhere his rifle cracked right next to me, which made me jump and this was followed by a whoop from him as the RPG gunner was dropped and that threat was no more. I remember calling out, 'Nice shot, Teddy.' Later, we both wondered if that bit would have been edited out of Ross Kemp's film but, in due course, it was nice to see that it had been included.

We kept up the pressure and eventually the Taliban began to realise they were clearly losing the battle, and so began to withdraw. Meanwhile, the FAC had been trying to give the circling Apaches a steer on to the enemy but they still could not see them. At this point, he lost his rag and told them to get out of his airspace, go home and retrain, which made me chuckle. Major Aston murmured, 'Mmm... this means we have no air cover.' However, Stewart explained that we had British Apaches en route, their call sign Ugly. I remembered hearing that callsign before, when Deano was wounded in Sangin, and thinking what a cool one it was. They would be arriving in five minutes, so we had to stay put until then, as Major Aston was not happy about moving on with no air cover.

We remained there, trying to keep eyes-on for any enemy while taking some sporadic fire from the building that our guys were hitting with their GPMGs. Teddy and I zapped the area with my rangefinder, but we could not really obtain a fix on anyone. At this point the British Apaches came in and we threw yet another smoke grenade which they spotted first time. We thought, 'Thank f.... for that' as Stewart directed them to the building Teddy and I were firing on. The boys in the Apaches gave it a good dose of 30mm cannon fire, giving it a really good going-over. Now that the immediate area was clear, Major Aston was happy to press on. To the north of us, A Company was coming up against some quite heavy resistance because the Taliban that were trying to escape from us, moving north as we had intended. They had to decide as to which was the lesser of two evils, us or A Company, as they were basically trapped between us and would have to decide which they were going to take on. Alternatively, they could play the joker card option, which was to cross the river and head for the Musa Qaleh wadi and safety.

After four hours of fighting, I only had around two litres of water left out of the six with which I had started the day. We found a well in the back of one of the compounds we had taken and started to refill our water bottles, putting puritabs in them. Teddy and I, and a couple of others, started talking to Ross Kemp and his crew, who asked us about Deano and what had happened. Teddy explained that he was our section commander and told them about his casevacing Deano under fire. They sat speechless and just said, 'Bloody hell! Well done!'

We crossed a field of crops, heading for another road. As we approached it, we could hear another contact start up far to the rear of us but it was quite a way back and no danger at all because, although we could hear the firing, there were none of the cracks and whistles you hear when you are involved in a fire fight. We turned around to look back and watched as Ross Kemp and all of his guys were sprinting up to us at full pelt with their heads down, and could not help smiling. We told them, 'You can get down here, lads', and they dived behind a small wall and immediately took up the foetal position as Teddy and I stood up and looked back.

At that point, we got a call over the radio and heard that Corporal Martin's section had been put into a group of compounds that had been shot up pretty badly and were as good as rubble now. The enemy were now being met by the ANA and at the same time 5 Platoon were starting to engage the Taliban that we were now chasing out of the area. I said to Teddy, 'You're a lance corporal, I'm a lance corporal – what do you want to do? Go and try to cut these boys off from the ANA or do you want to catch up with 5 Platoon and try to give them cover?' Teddy's first instinct was to go and do the guys up in our area with the ANA and I agreed. I got on the radio and told Major Aston of our plan and gave a grid reference of where we were going to be. He responded, saying no dramas and happy hunting, so we found ourselves negotiating the rubble of shattered compounds to find ourselves a position. We were joined by Private Medlock who had a GPMG and found himself up on the same bit of ledge as Teddy, below which I positioned myself.

After about five or ten minutes, Teddy started firing and then Medlock joined in with the GPMG. Teddy shouted down that they had around fifteen Taliban out in the open, fleeing from the ANA, and said they were about 300 metres away moving west to east. I extracted my map and GPS and plotted a six-figure grid reference of where they

88

were and then used the radio to report our contact and the location. As they fled, the Taliban must have thought they were safe after breaking contact with the ANA, so suddenly to come up against a GPMG and a sniper was not great news for them. Teddy got three kills in the end and Medlock scored two, so we killed a third of their number.

Corporal Martin had obviously heard what was going on, so I briefed him fully on the situation. Teddy came down to join us and mentioned that Medlock had done well, earning him some well-deserved praise from Corporal Martin. His grin was visible from England, so it was good for morale. Teddy then reloaded his magazines before we pushed on up to find ourselves behind Major Aston, Ross Kemp and his crew whom we accompanied through some more compounds where we halted and the decision was made to wait and regroup. While we waited, we found ourselves in a little room with Ross Kemp and his guys, along with some mortar men, and it was here that I had a good chat with him. We stayed there for a good half an hour or more, being resupplied with ammunition and a few more bottles of water each. The water was particularly welcome because we had been in contact for some six or seven hours and I had almost run out. Thereafter, we prepared to join Corporal Parker's section once more as we went forward.

We moved off and in our minds it soon became a bit like a Vietnam War movie again as we snaked through fields and crops. I turned a corner and froze as I found myself facing a Taliban bunker some seven or eight metres away. Fortunately, it was unoccupied as otherwise I would not have stood a chance. After that we uncovered a network of bunkers whose positions we logged for the engineers who were following us, so that they could demolish them.

We pushed on and eventually came across a place where we found a heavy blood trail on the ground together with a large number of AK-47 spent casings. I bent down to feel one of them and found it was still warm. This indicated that we were close behind some enemy who were retreating with dead or wounded, so we increased our pace to try and catch up with them. In the distance, we could hear A Company having a battle royal with the Taliban who were trying everything to break through but without success, leaving them trapped between our two companies.

By this time, we were all now shattered after fighting for so many hours. My back was absolutely killing me under the massive weight of the kit I was carrying, and I was suffering from really very bad prickly heat all over it. I took my day sack off and grabbed the bottom of my shirt and squeezed it, literally wringing the sweat out of it. My back felt like it was almost scaly so I asked Teddy to take a look to see if I had what felt like a huge, painful scab across my back – there wasn't but he confirmed that it was incredibly red. All of us were feeling the strain, including Private Medlock who earlier had done so well but was starting to get really faint too. After all, by this time we had been on the go for some ten hours in intense heat, carrying massive loads.

The sun was now going down and it was about time to move out, so we cut right and got back down into a drainage ditch heading back to the 611 road, doubling back on ourselves and heading for the compounds we had occupied previously where Teddy had killed the RPG gunner. We were moving fast, which was agony for me but I just had to grin and bear it. Last light came, so we had to stop and don our night viewing kit. Shortly afterwards, we came upon an elderly Afghan locking up his building and but it transpired he had come to collect his Quran and a few other items, so we sent him on his way.

We continued patrolling back; by now we had been on the ground for something like thirteen or fourteen hours. Before we reached the compound where we were to stay for the night, we had to clear them again, but this time on a totally green code because, although we needed to do this as a precaution, we also did not want to let the Taliban know exactly where we were by firing needlessly.

We reached the compound where Lieutenant Seal-Coon told us that a stag system to protect us all had already been set up and so we did not need to stag on, but he wanted us to sleep on the roof just in case anything kicked off. We would be there with night vision gear to help in seconds up there. By this time the temperature had dropped down to something like fifteen to twenty degrees, which to us felt bloody freezing; with no cloud cover and a wind, we were shivering like crazy.

We were freezing, with no cloud cover and wind coming in too. It took only a few minutes before we both realised that the only situation was to huddle in the spoons position. We both groaned and thought, 'Piss off, I'd rather be cold.' But as the wind continued to whip across, we both just thought, 'Bugger it!' Uncomfortable as it was for our male pride, it was better than freezing to death – just. To be fair, it didn't really work because when I was asleep Teddy would be shivering and wake me up, and then it would be vice-versa. Eventually, I had enough and, picking up my rifle, headed downstairs. At least I could have a cigarette there which would have been impossible on the roof because it would have been like a neon light flashing to the Taliban saying 'British Troops here.' I looked in all of the rooms, which were full of snoring soldiers, for something to keep us warm and finally found an old blanket. It was full of crap and stank of horse shit, but I thought it would at least give us the warmth to enable us to get some shut-eye. Teddy and I lay there slightly warmer, but could feel the fleas and whatever else that seemed to be crawling around the blanket on us. In the end, we just grit our teeth, closed our eyes and went to sleep, totally knackered, on a roof in Afghanistan. Happy days!

Later, when being debriefed, we learned that all the Taliban bunkers that we came across were destroyed. There were more, packed full of ammunition and RPGs, but by pure luck we had entered Jusyalay about 600 metres to the south of these positions, literally a stone's throw away from carnage. If we had continued with the original plan, we would have come out on top of these bunkers and would have suffered heavy casualties. These positions were well sited, a perfect killing ground for the Taliban.

CHAPTER 12

Aftermath

Thankfully, not a great deal happened that night and we rose early. I had rolled away from the blanket and, although the sun was bright when it rose, it was still cold. At least my clothes were now dry, but because of the sheer amount of sweating done the previous day, the back of my shirt was like cardboard and had a white chalky residue all around the edges from where the salt that had crystallised from the sweat. Although I didn't realise it at the time, this would compound the problems with my back, which was still hurting quite a bit, when more sweat would mix in with the salt and grime from the previous day and rub into my already raw skin making it total agony as I donned my day sack, weapons and kit. I had now been wearing this one set of clothes for around two or three weeks, albeit I had managed to borrow a few pairs of socks.

I came off the roof to go downstairs and have a cigarette, so as not give away our position. It was around 4.00 am in the morning and I sat on the steps leading from the roof into the main building. A few of the guys were beginning to wake up too and someone said that it was 'stand to' in half an hour – we would man our positions wearing all of our kit and be ready to repel any attack. I went back to the roof after I finished my fag and shook Teddy awake, letting him know that 'stand to' was soon. We made sure our kit was ready, put on our body armour and I checked that the fresh battery was fitted to my radio.

Following 'stand down', we found out that we were to be working with 5 Platoon alongside Sergeant Caneper. Yesterday we had pushed on down the route between the 611 road and the Helmand River and found all of the enemy bunkers that had since been blown up by the engineers. Today we were going back to check that the Taliban were not trying to re-infiltrate the area. If necessary, we would take the fight to them again; no one had really done this previously or stayed for long periods of time in the Green Zone. If the Taliban did want to stick around they would have to throw us out, which was not going to happen.

We moved through a field, halting by a bridge that ran over quite a wide canal with substantial tree cover over the top. Teddy recognised the spot and kept looking around before finally saying, 'Over here JC.' I went over and saw a puddle of congealed blood, but no body. The Taliban never leave any of their fallen behind, but we grinned anyway. This may seem callous but, if you consider what warfare is really like, take into account our friends being blown up or shot and remember the Taliban were trying to kill us, perhaps our feelings were understandable.

We moved forward again; even though the sun had only been up for a few hours, it was hot with the temperature in the 30s. As we patrolled forward, we came across an old school and then a mosque where the Taliban had hidden the day before. We couldn't gain access to it, to check it for weapons because it was padlocked, and we were not permitted to touch it as it was a religious building. The previous day it had been full of fully armed Taliban shooting at us but, although we could have flattened it with our air and mortar assets, we could not do so. We looked around the area, but there was nothing to be seen with no one around at all to talk to. It was quite a dense Green Zone area with trees overhanging thickly and little houses or assorted buildings set about the place in amongst the trees, irrigation ditches and fields.

We continued patrolling, moving for around five or six hours which really took its toll. Patrolling in that kind of heat was both physically and mentally exhausting, especially in that type of dense close country. We were having to concentrate so hard on what was going on around us and be totally aware of our own guys, as we could have come under attack at anytime at all. We needed to check all of the variables including a constant assessment of the ground around us, in order to be able to instinctively take cover towards the most appropriate place if we came under fire. We also had to be vigilant as we passed people, buildings, dense treelines and so on, all of which were potential threats. If I saw a stick poking up out of the ground, I would be asking myself if it might be a marker for the Taliban and if we were about to walk into an ambush. We were aware that the Russians had left large numbers of mines behind and the Taliban had dug many of them up, sometimes stacking them two or three on top of each other and rigging them so they would detonate under the weight of one man. These were not anti-personnel personnel but anti-tank mines, and we had not been issued with mine detectors because they still had not arrived in theatre at this point, so the need to be aware of even slightly disturbed earth was crucial.

Around midday, we came to an area that contained a few buildings sited pretty close together. We halted in these for a while as the temperature was now hitting 45 degrees, it now being the beginning of June in Afghanistan. We needed to let the worst of the heat die down but, at the same time, could not just take the kit off our backs and have a kip. We had to stay alert against any potential attack as we were so deep in the Green Zone that there was no vehicle support. While the guys got up on the roofs, Teddy and I went and filled up our water bottles from the well. We were always issued with tablets in our ration tablets to purify water. Having filled our bottles, we would drop the tablets into them and shake them up pretty well. This saved us having to boil water and then wait for it to cool down, which took forever. Apart from the water tasting a bit like chlorine, it was at least cold which was welcome in the heat. We all cleaned ourselves up a bit and washed the sand and grit out of our hair and off our faces before making our way back to our respective compounds.

We all had our own little rooms in the compound and Teddy and I were bunked in with Sergeant Chris Caneper. We got our heads down for a little while as there were sentries on the roofs. We also took some food on board. I had my favourite boil-in-the-bag: chicken and mushroom with carbonara sauce. I had been carrying it in the uppermost compartment of my day sack, closest to the sun, in an attempt to warm it through, because we were unable to cook where we were. The result was a sort of lukewarm goo, which was pretty disgusting and nothing like the veal steak and mushrooms I had acquired from the Canadians. But at least it was food and I badly needed some to keep going.

After a while we pushed on, positioning ourselves up on roofs and patrolling but nothing happened. The area was totally deserted, with no sign of any movement. We eventually arrived at the compound we had occupied the day before, which also had a well where everyone filled their water bottles while also taking the opportunity to consume as much liquid as possible. Colour Sergeant Bill Shand had done what we call a NAAFI run and had squared us away with a large quantity of provisions, including cigarettes, cans of coke and Haribo sweets. He had it delivered by Chinook helicopter, having managed to sweet talk one of the RAF loadmasters into putting it on with a load of ammunition and other supplies. This was hugely appreciated because we knew that getting this stuff out in the Green Zone was a luxury and not a necessity.

We had been on the go for another full day in this heat with only three or four hours sleep. Sergeant Caneper stood there with this load in front of him, as everyone swarmed around the bounty, eyeing up the Haribo and coke. In the end he just said, 'Will you all just f... off and let me sort this out.' Quite funny but understandable that, after days of drinking chlorine flavoured water and running around in stinking clothes, tempers were becoming short.

One of the medics also came around asking if we were all okay. One of the guys that had just joined us and was brand new was saying, 'My feet are just killing me.' We all just said, 'Come on, son, get a grip.' He really insisted he had a problem and so the medic took a look, along with the rest of us. We pulled his boots off and found his feet had gone totally white. He had been wearing nylon socks instead of the issued cotton ones we all wore, so while we would be losing a pint of sweat through our feet every three or four hours, he had been losing unbelievable amounts. The result was a very bad case of 'trench foot.'

The phrase, 'trench foot' originated in the First World War, during which where soldiers' feet would constantly be underwater and soaking wet for so long that they would eventually start to rot. This is incredibly painful as the skin starts to break off in lumps. I know how painful it is, as I had once suffered from trench foot when I was a new guy back in the UK.

This guy must have kept quiet for days because the state of his feet was really shocking. The medic was trying to be sympathetic but began bollocking him for not raising the problem earlier. The section commander had to step in and tell the medic to back off because the guy was new. He then went through the guy's kit, finding more nylon socks and telling him if he ever caught him wearing them again he would be put on a charge. Fortunately, he also had the issued socks that we all wore, so the medic delved into his pack and pulled out a big tub of foot powder, which is very potent stuff. He smothered the guy's feet in it as well as pouring it into his new issue socks so that when he woke up and put his boots on, he would get a full day's coating. We then carried the guy over to a building where he was told to keep off his feet for the rest of the night, although if the shit hit the fan and we had to move out quickly he would have to grin and bear it and put on his boots like the rest of us. He was a new guy and inexperienced and obviously thought he was doing himself a favour wearing sporty style clothing. As he learnt quite quickly and the hard way, there are good reasons why what we do most of the time in the Army is tried and tested and bloody well works.

After all the fun and games with the feet, we all went back out to the well and filled up with water and splashed about cleaning ourselves up and cooled down a bit, the sentries up on the roofs meanwhile keeping a watchful eye on the surroundings. By this time, Sergeant Caneper had worked everything out regarding the goodies and supplies, imposing a limit on each item so it did not become a free-for-all and everyone got equal amounts. Everyone of course ordered the maximum of everything and the smokers stocked up on cigarettes. It was excellent for morale and the sugar in the 'full fat coke' and the Haribo sweets was a much-needed boost to our energy levels too.

We all had another boil-in-the-bag, and I swapped a number of my other meals with some of the guys, so I had a decent amount of my favourite chicken and mushroom for going forward. I got my head down and slept for a little while and woke up to find a can of coke with a bag of Haribo sweets, so I walked outside and asked Teddy whose they were. He told me that there had been a few left over, so he had squared them away for me. We sat and had a smoke and a can of coke together, chatting for a while until 'stand to' was called and we all got kitted up and ready to go. 'Stand down' was called after a while and we retired to our sleeping quarters.

We patrolled right through the Green Zone and all the way up to the Helmand River. There were a few compounds there, with a large open field with a long treeline running across it. There was a compound there, with another just behind it and a third in the distance beyond. Beyond the river was a kind of canyon that opened up, reminding me of films of Ayers Rock in Australia. We could also see big high yellow cliffs on the other side of the wadi with a kind of valley which stretched into the distance: this was the Musa Qaleh wadi and the back door to the Taliban's main stronghold.

We went across to the compounds and knocked on the door; there was no answer, so we kicked the door in. On entering, we found a family inside: a man along with his son, aged about twenty years old, his wife who was totally covered in a burqa, and some children. They all shrieked and screamed at first, but we called our interpreter in and told him to tell them that we were British forces and were there to help. We asked if they had seen any Taliban. The man told us that they had left a few days ago and gone via the Musa Qaleh wadi to Musa Qaleh. We pressed him politely, asking he was sure, but he insisted the Taliban had gone. We then asked if we could use his compound for the next few hours. At first he moaned a bit, but was soon relatively accommodating after receiving some compensation in the form of US dollars, telling us to help ourselves. We went out the back to his garden near the Helmand River which was shaded by extremely dense trees. We had been patrolling for a good six hours and my back was on fire, so it was good to drop the daysack, take on some food and water. Meanwhile, a couple of WMIKs and a Pinzgauer had succeeded in driving down and getting through to us.

In view of the fact that there no Taliban in the near vicinity, Major Mick Aston decided to hold a *shura* with the elders of the area. We all got ourselves up to the edge of the river and, while we were waiting, Ross Kemp came over with his camera crew and talked with Teddy as we had told him about Teddy risking his life to save Deano. We sat with him for a while, showing him how to zap a rangefinder laser at a number of potential targets including some upturned boats.

Shortly afterwards, I fell asleep but was woken by the CSM saying, 'Do you want your R & R?' He told me that we were to leave soon and for me to get my kit on, get loaded up and ready to move out. There were the inevitable calls of, 'You lucky bastard!' We all received the same amount of mid-tour R & R, so I enjoyed telling them that I would see them later and to f... off. I dived into my day sack and gave Teddy some of my cigarettes, thereafter dishing out the rest of my boil-in-the bags to the lads. Teddy said that he would walk me out. It was slightly strange in the sense that in normal civilian circumstances this just wouldn't be appropriate, but we grabbed each others thumbs and palms and we turned and hugged. I don't care what anyone says, because that was totally normal and totally appropriate to our situation. He told me to enjoy myself and I told him to keep his head down, stay low, move fast and all that stuff.

With that, I jumped into the vehicle as Major Aston had finished his meeting with the elders. There seemed to be large numbers of people around as we drove out of there up to a massive hilltop where the Recce Platoon and a few other vehicles were stationed. We were quite high up, so could see down on to the Green Zone and the Musa Qaleh wadi. From this vantage point I could see clearly where we had come, how far we had patrolled and cleared and it was a really good sense of achievement. I recognised a few of the Marines that were tending to their Vikings and they asked me how it was in there and I described it to them, telling them of my kill and of Teddy taking the enemy RPG gunner's head off.

AFTERMATH

I met up with Pete Tointon and he told me in no uncertain terms that I looked like shit and I agreed by saying, 'You're not wrong.' All of us were being pulled out on R & R, among them Josh Lee, OD and a few others were in the same state. I was offered something to eat and refused, saying I didn't fancy yet another boil-in-the bag, until the guy mentioned that he had the last of a few Canadian meals, including veal steak in mushroom sauce.

That night, I slept up on a ridge after talking to Colour Sergeant Snow and the next day we prepared to fly back to Camp Bastion with Ross Kemp and his crew. Before jumping on, we had to carry a stretcher laden with a pile of stuff to the Chinook. The nightmare was that the helicopter landed about four or five hundred metres away, so four of us had to carry this stretcher over to them. The blades were going full bore and kicking up dust as we ran, tripping over rocks and blinded by clouds of dust, towards the aircraft. We made it just as I thought my arm was about to be dislocated. Almost blinded by the sand which had been kicked up, but with a feeling of relief and elation, I sat in the aircraft as it lifted off thinking that at last I was flying home, albeit I would be returning in a few weeks.

The flight to Camp Bastion was not long. As we landed, Ross Kemp turned and told me that he hoped we had a great break, which was good of him. We took ourselves over to the company lines where all the quartermaster stores were. I remember noticing about four or five new guys who had obviously just arrived: their clothing perfect, their skin white with sun cream all over their noses. I stood near them, in filthy kit, stinking to high heaven with a sweatband wrapped around my dripping head and my clothes in shreds. God knows what they must have thought.

Lance Corporal Coolage, better known to all as 'Coolio', came out and told us that he would look after our weapons if we wanted to go to the cookhouse for some food. We lost no time in getting ourselves across there and were soon getting stuck into croissants, sausage and egg, and cold orange juice. This was heaven, five star treatment. Breakfast over, we went to strip and clean our weapons but the inevitable happened. After eating boil-in-the-bags for over a month, the sudden intake of fresh food had a dire effect on us. The toilets were far better than the thunderboxes out in the FOBs but it was still like sitting in a sauna. To top it off, there were no toilet seats to sit on, just hot metal – still the graffiti on the walls made for interesting reading.

After the weapons had been cleaned, they were going to be serviced thoroughly before being reissued to us on our return from R & R, so I stripped and cleaned my rifle three times before I handed it in. I must admit that it felt weird not wearing body armour, sitting in a plastic chair with a pair of three-quarter length trousers on, with an iPod plugged in to my ears as I cleaned my weapon. I wrote out a list of all the ammunition that I handed in, then I tied it all up and put a name tag on, so everyone knew what was what when we came back.

Finally, I reached the point that I had dreamt of for such a long time – shower time. I stood under the shower for what seemed hours and it was the best feeling in the world, I watching the water run off me and form a pool of solid brown obscuring my feet. Eventually, I came out and collected a packet of cigarettes from my box in the ISO container. I also extracted my DVD player and saw a note from Scotty, who had left it from when he had gone on R & R. It read, 'Hi JC, borrowed this to watch porn on, left it in for you though.' I then telephoned home and spoke to Annie, before writing letters to people to let them know I was coming home. I had to wait for one more day before flying out. My R & R was to start on 5 June, so as it was the 4th I began to pack away all of my kit. At the same time, I unpacked a clean uniform ready for my return.

CHAPTER 13

R & R

We flew from Bastion to the American base at Kandahar, and from there directly back to the UK where it was surprisingly warm as we disembarked at Brize Norton. I had telephoned Annie from Kandahar and gave her the time for the family to pick me up, but I got it all wrong and they were an hour late. Eventually, my mum and Annie turned up and there was of course a lot of excitement. It was just such a fantastic feeling to be home as forty-eight hours earlier I had been in the field taking incoming fire; now here I was in the arms of my loved ones.

We arrived home in Peterborough and later that day Annie and I went over to my flat in Werrington where we spent some time before returning to my mum's place where my brother Ben was waiting for me. We then all headed for our 'local', the Harrier pub in Gunthorpe, where we met a group of our mates. My mum had been giving them all updates while I was away, so when I walked in you can imagine it was a case of lots of people shouting, 'Hey, he's back! He's back!' Every time I produced my wallet, everyone told me to put it away and I remember a guy called Jeremy kept shaking my hand and slapping my back so hard it actually hurt, telling me how much he appreciated what we were doing and thanking me for it. I felt so touched and really grateful and of course tried to play it all down, but all I could manage to say, 'You're welcome.' I kept trying to divert the attention away from me and tell them that the guys were still out there, but it was really nice to see such appreciation of what we were trying to do. It was a wonderful and very surreal experience and one I will never forget.

I was lucky enough to be back on my mum's birthday and she had organised for us all to go out into the city centre to a Chinese restaurant called Imperial Bento's, a massive place that had only just opened. After that, we moved on to a nearby pub called the College Arms for a few more pints to see the night out before heading home. It was a great night which we all really enjoyed and I ended up collapsing on my mum's sofa, waking up on the following morning with that 'Where the hell am I?' feeling before remembering that I was home on R&R.

I needed to go to see Deano and so made my way to Birmingham and Selly Oak. On arrival at the hospital, I walked round the wards until I found where he was but, as I was a little bit early, I went to buy a card from the gift shop. As I entered and started walking up the ward, I simply did not know what to think or say. I could see wounded men with bandages around their legs and limbs missing and thought, 'Shit! This is where we end up!' It was an enormous eye-opener which made me feel so sad for the guys who had been doing their jobs and had simply been unlucky. It also made me feel incredibly fortunate to be healthy and alive, and so far to have come out the other end unscathed. As bad as that may seem, I guess it is human nature to think through what might have happened to you and then thank your lucky stars, so that's what I did. I had read in the papers before about Muslim women attacking the lads in the wards and it made me feel sick. Surely, if they had become legal British citizens then it should make that kind of behaviour some form of treason. The extra security was clearly evident.

As I rounded the corner towards Deano, his face lit up, despite the fact that he was still being heavily sedated to deal with the actual pain of his injuries. I don't know, but I guess a familiar and unexpected face always helps.

I shook his hand, which felt slightly fragile, so I was careful not to pull his arm off. I sat down beside him and started to show him his books and stuff that I had managed to bring back from Afghanistan. He slowly opened them without speaking and smiled as he flicked through the pages. As he was doing this, his girlfriend came into the room and said, 'Hi' and asked who I was. I told her I was JC and that

I was on R&R before explaining that I was Deano's second-in-command in Afghanistan.

Deano gestured towards a pen and notebook on the side and I passed it over. He very slowly wrote that he could not talk or hear anything and pointed. So I started to write down initial things like, 'How are you doing mate?' Thereafter we had a conversation via paper and pen because it was the only way we could communicate with each other. He was deaf as a result of the RPG explosion, added to which he was pretty heavily sedated so it took a while for him to be able to write his replies to my questions, especially after having to decipher my terrible handwriting. He asked what had been happening and, as I began to explain, his parents turned up so after the introductions, I told them all everything I could to the best of my knowledge about what had happened to him, because he couldn't remember any of it apart from the explosion. I reminded him that he had been covered in fuel and the fact that he had bravely taken his body armour off to enable him to continue to fight, but he couldn't remember doing so.

Shortly afterwards our old RSM, WO1 Tony Buff, turned up as he had been posted to Selly Oak as a welfare officer and was doing his rounds. He asked me how I had got to the hospital, so I told him that I had travelled over in my own car. He asked why I had not asked for official transport to drive me down and I said that I had not even thought about that but just obtained the address of the hospital and made my way to it. I could have caught a train, using a rail warrant, but that was not really important as I just wanted to see Deano and check he was okay. I would have paid for ten tanks of petrol to see him as he was my team commander and my mate. It was good to see him smile as he read my card. At that point I started to get ready to leave, as I did not want to out stay my welcome. He wrote down for me to look after the guys and I replied, 'Of course I will. No dramas.'

After shaking hands with everyone, I went outside. I must admit that I had to choke back the emotion as it had been so hard to see Deano like that. He was the heart and soul of every occasion, the party animal and larger than life, so it was terrible to see him in this state and I felt guilt and sadness.

I drove back home and, as I arrived, I could smell that Annie had been cooking. I walked in and said, 'Hi!.' At that point I had a few tears with Annie as I thought about what had happened and the fact that I usually worked with Teddy and so it really should have been me in that ambush. Annie told me that Deano was just doing his job and leading his section, and no one could have known what was going to happen; indeed she reminded me that it might have been me that got hurt in place of someone else after I had switched to being a mortar man, so it was wrong to blame myself. She was right, of course, and I guess such emotions are simply one of the many mental challenges of being a soldier on active service.

A few days before I was due to go back, I decided to throw a party at my flat in Werrington and so set about buying in all the meat for the barbecue. As it was a beautiful sunny day, we set up a gazebo in my postage stamp sized garden at my flat. I recruited the help of my mate, 'Dodgy' Dave, who is an absolute legend on the barbecue and I would challenge anyone to find a better man at donning the apron and cooking a barbie. As his job was a plumber and he had come straight from work, his girlfriend had brought his clothes across for him and he used my shower to have a wash and change and then he was straight out to sort the barbie.

People started to arrive: Jodie, obviously Annie, my brother, Bones and Leanne, Cheryl, Hailey, Rob and Michaela, Ozzy and Becky, Leah and so on. We made the most of my flat and garden, with fairy lights strung up in the gazebo. Everyone ate great food and got nicely pissed, laughing and talking, which was great.

Suddenly Rob, who had been drinking Vodka and Red Bull and had been fine earlier, changed and sort of snapped. In fairness to him, he took it outside as he continued to go totally nuts. I was a bit worried because he was a bit close to my neighbour's car, but this was all very strange because it was just not like him at all, so I sent Ozzy outside to see if he could calm him down and find out what the hell it was. It was no use, as he just became worse and neighbours started to come out as we tried to restrain him because he was lashing out as we attempted to calm him down and prevent from doing himself and anyone else any damage.

The trouble was that we all ended up on the floor in a scuffle and the next thing we knew the police had arrived with blue lights flashing and sirens wailing, then jumping out and running towards us with batons fully extended. We all jumped up and were saying, 'Whoa, whoa! What's all this for? I said to the police, 'Calm down fellas, this is a storm in a tea cup.' They told us in no uncertain terms to get off Rob and ran towards him. I just said, 'What's this all about? I live here,' and pointed to my flat. 'We're just having a party, we're all mates.' Meanwhile, I was trying to calm Rob down and help him because he had had a bit too much to drink.

The coppers told us that they had received a telephone call reporting three guys kicking the crap out of one another on his own. Of course we all laughed and said, 'No, no. He's a mate and he's clearly drunk and got all upset and we were trying to calm him down, restrain him and find out what the hell he's upset about. He hasn't caused any damage or harm apart from disturbing my leaving party and is just a bit upset about something.' The policeman turned to me and said, 'Oh right. So this is your party, is it?.' I thought, 'Oh f..., here we go' and began the process of giving a statement and confirming details.

At the end of it all, they slapped handcuffs on Rob and put him in the van, while a growing mass of neighbours looked on. This is a pretty quiet part of Werrington and it certainly was not normal for police to be storming the street, so literally everyone was out and standing around staring. Rob had now been packed off and his girlfriend had also left, so we went back inside. Annie was obviously quite upset, saying that it was all right for me because I was off again, but she now had to live in this area with everyone looking at her, judging her and thinking we were some form of chavs. I could see her point and said, 'Right, I'm not having that' and said that I would go and talk to them. They were all still out there, so I just addressed the massed crowd and said, 'Look, this was clearly nothing to do with Annie, it was simply a guy who drank too much and we were as shocked as everyone else, but these things happen and it's just one of those things.'

The police, of course, realised pretty quickly that this was the case and put Rob in a cell for the night to sober up and let him go on the following morning with no charges. The rest of us meanwhile went back and continued to drink and party until the wee early hours of around 4.00 or 5.00 am without further incident. Apart from that little bit of excitement, it was good humoured, a great laugh and a fitting send-off. Annie and I collapsed into bed when everyone eventually left and we drifted off to sleep, only to awake needing the essential proper breakfast and got on with it.

All too soon it was time to head back to Afghanistan. I decided that I would take my car back to the barracks as I would be back again in three months, and so my car should be fine there. We said our farewells and there were a few tears and many cuddles, especially as I was far more aware of the dangers than previously. I then left on the long journey back to Elizabeth barracks in Pirbright, Surrey, feeling very lonely after two weeks of being with my loved ones and friends.

Following our arrival, the first thing for those of us who had been on R & R was to go and sign for all of our kit. We spotted Macca, who had been shot just underneath the armour plate in his body armour, hobbling along on a walking stick. We shook his hand and he told us that we really should try to avoid getting shot because, in his words, 'It f...ing hurts.' I told him that I remembered seeing the state of him on the stretcher and that I needed no persuading – I did not want to be shot.

A lot of the barracks were still being re-furbished and so I took over a bed in B Company's lines and slept for a while before ordering a Chinese takeaway and playing poker well into the night. Soon the minibus arrived to take us back to RAF Brize Norton, where we were processed in the same way as my initial trip to Afghanistan, before embarking on the aircraft.

We arrived at Kandahar and stayed overnight before boarding a Hercules C-130 for the flight to Camp Bastion and the pods on Camp 501 for a couple of days while we waited for the helicopters to fly us out to Nowzad. B Company had also come off MOGs after Operation LASTAY KULANG and was now based at Nowzad, minus 5 and 6 Platoons who had been involved in another operation, GHARTSI-GHAR, which took place during 20 June to 5 July. The number of attacks by the Taliban were on the increase and intimidation of the locals was spreading, so the aim of Operation GHARTSI-GHAR was to rectify this situation by pushing the Taliban back even further and preventing them from re-infiltrating the Green Zone around Sangin, thus taking the pressure off the city itself. The plan was to allow the locals to be able to move back into the city without having the threat of the Taliban on their doorstep all the time.

The initial stages of the operation were recorded as follows in the Battalion's tour magazine:

Both A and B Companies made long approach marches through the Green Zone at night, in order to be in position to block the enemy's potential escape route across the Helmand River. After an almost 12 km night approach march, both companies were in almost continuous contact for the whole of the following day. They remained in the Green Zone and the fire fight lasted for nine days. Once again, large numbers of the enemy were killed with far fewer escaping this time. As an act of desperation, the Taliban used a twelve-year-old boy to place an IED in the Sangin bazaar which detonated, killing the young boy and two policemen. This single incident was the turning point for public opinion as it caused outrage, resulting in the amount of information about the Taliban received from the local population being quadrupled. Most importantly, the Taliban's perception that the area was a safe haven for them was shattered and the locals began to realise that there was an alternative to suffering intimidation. Reconstruction efforts were boosted following this operation with significantly more locals coming forward with proposals for a number of projects, particularly for irrigation projects and improvements.

5 and 6 Platoons were in the Green Zone in the thick of the main part

of Operation GHARTSI-GHAR. Meanwhile 7 Platoon was in Nowzad and the FSG was on ANP Hill, which was just outside the town but still provided 360 degree views around the entire area due to its elevation. The FSG could see exactly where the platoons were and knew exactly the location of the Taliban.

While we were waiting in Camp Bastion, we helped to sort a mountain of mail for distribution. A few of the guys from C Company arrived back from their R & R at this time and, having been in the company, I knew a few of them. One of them was a guy called Tony Rawson whose nickname was 'Nicey' the reason was as simple as it sounds: he was one of the nicest blokes you could be fortunate enough to meet and would go out of his way to help newly joined soldiers joining the company and not knowing anyone, which is always a bit daunting. I also saw Si Mercer who showed me all his photographs of what C Company's FSG had been getting up to in Kajaki in the north of the province. It was good to catch up with them and to find out about Robbo, Tom, Dan and Cas and all the guys in the snipers and FSG.

Colour Sergeant Bill Shand had told us that it would be a few days before we were flown out, but that later that day he appeared and informed us that we were moving out immediately. We swiftly packed our kit and shortly afterwards were on the flight to Nowzad which proved uneventful. On its final approach, the helicopter swept in low and let off a couple of flares, landing us in a small wadi just behind ANP Hill. So there I was, a couple of weeks of peace now ended and the next three months of this tour of operations to get through, which would prove to be far from plain sailing.

CHAPTER 14

Nowzad –
The Ghost Town

The Chinook helicopter flew off, the downdraught covering us in dust. We took up defensive positions in the wadi and waited and waited, then waited some more. After a while, we began to think, 'Oh shit. Where are our guys?' There were ten or fifteen of us, carrying bags of mail as well as our own personal kit and full bergens. The trouble is, when a Chinook lands and then flies off, the Taliban know that something or someone has just been dropped off at that spot.

Eventually, we observed a Pinzgauer driving up towards accompanied by some WMIKs from the FSG. They pulled up and we all jumped in before setting off along a dusty track that took us back into the Nowzad district centre. Our base there had now been renamed FOB Gray, after Private Chris Gray who was sadly killed not far from there on 13 April right at the start of the tour. Being back in the UK for even as little as two weeks had de-acclimatised us and we found it bloody hot and were soon desperate for some water. On arrival at the FOB, we unloaded all the kit and headed for the main HQ building where there was a big fridge with lovely ice cold water. I discarded my helmet and body armour before wandering off for a look around our new base which was not bad at all. There was even a television with BFBS (British Forces Broadcasting Service) that provided us with BBC One, Channel 4, a sports channel and a music channel along with a few others that no one really watched. There were also a few benches with tables nearby piled high with books for everyone to read and another table with 'highbrow' magazines like *NUTS*, *Zoo* and others. There were also three text link terminals, so we could securely send texts back home which was useful because Nowzad was a little out of the way. Mail came once a week if we were lucky, more likely every fortnight when we would receive quite a good bundle of letters that was swapped for our outgoing mail.

I went over to the Operations Room and spoke to everyone there, blagging on about my R & R. Other than that, I had nothing to do, so watched a bit of television and chatted on with a few people, finding out what had been going on in the area in my absence. Ross Kemp and his crew had now finished their filming and returned to the UK, and it was back to normal life in Afghanistan for me.

After a while, the WMIKs returned with the FSG guys who all lived up on ANP Hill, which is an old fort on a feature that looks over and dominates the entire Nowzad area. Nowzad itself lies in a massive area of flat terrain and is surrounded by mountains, like crocodile ridge and also is populated by lots of little villages. One of them is called Karizi Afga, which we called Crazy Afghan, while other places had strange names like Jedi, which of course reminded me of the film *Star Wars*, but all in all the terrain was beautiful.

Along with some defensive positions constructed by the Russians, ANP Hill itself has a shrine and crypt built in to it, which I was told dated all the way back to the days of Genghis Khan and that there were generations of important people buried under there. I am not a hundred per cent sure if this is true, but inevitably there were rumours that the place was haunted.

I met the FSG guys and the normal high fives, hugs and catch-up took place. There was a real bond within our ranks that probably will never be replicated during the rest of our lives. I was hoping to see Teddy, but he had just flown out for his R & R and we had literally just missed each other. He had ended up taking Deano's R & R slot as he had arrived a couple of weeks later in the tour, so all the good slots had gone. This would have normally meant that, by the time his came up, he would have gone back about five or six weeks before the whole tour was finished, and then only to fly back out for a few weeks. It would have firstly been a bit pointless, but also a bit of a bastard, because it's a long hard slog without a break for around five months. Scotty was back from R & R, so it was us two as the sniper team. Having sorted ourselves out, we drove up to ANP Hill where I acquainted myself with my new home for the next six weeks or so before sending a bluey off to Annie. It was 15 July, right in the middle of summer in Afghanistan, so the temperature was well into the fifties and absolutely roasting – too hot to sit by a pool with your shorts on, let alone fight wearing full kit and body armour.

We received an orientation and brief from Snowy, who was now a WO2. I now had to stop addressing him as 'Colour Sergeant' and call him 'Sir' instead. Scotty showed me to my room where I could not stand upright because it was so low. It was like accommodation of the First World War, extending along the face of the hill and dug in underneath razor wire with corrugated iron sheets overhead. Within arm's reach of the beds were firing ports. I took Teddy's bed and Scotty was in the same hole next to me; further down the line was the rest of the FSG. In our hole we had a .338 rifle and an L96. We also had our laser rangefinders and two Leopold scopes, so we were pretty well kitted out.

There was a kitchen area round the back, with chicken wire fencing that had been made into a hut with hessian wrapped around it, so we could cook for ourselves up on the hill. The trouble was that it wasn't as though we all sat down to dinner for our three square meals a day – we all ate 'on the fly' or when we could, so would end up having snacks and occasionally a big proper meal if we had sufficient time to cook one. There were shower facilities, which consisted of a hole in the ground covered by a parachute on top of six-foot pickets. We also had a makeshift gym, equipped with a rowing machine, chin pull-up bars, weights that were containers of various description filled with sand, and a bench press where we used a bunch of six-foot pickets. One of these pickets on its own does not weigh too much but when you stack half a dozen of them together, they are very heavy. We also had a satellite phone up on the hill on which we could call home on when the signal was strong enough, this depending on where the satellite was at the time. We used to look up at the sky at night to try and spot its faint white outline of continuous light overhead, the air being so clear out there with no pollution.

Not a great deal happened in Nowzad because the local population had left due to the presence of the Taliban only some 700 metres away from us in the Green Zone. They watched us every step of the way and if we went to within around 300 metres of them, they would lay ambushes and subject us to heavy fire. When British forces first arrived in the area, the Paras and the Gurkhas had to deal with the Taliban coming right up to the perimeter fence and throwing grenades over the top. Our battalion was tasked with breaking this situation and A Company had achieved it during an operation that took place while I was on R & R. We succeeded in freeing up some of the open ground to create a buffer zone between us and the Taliban, and to allow us more freedom of movement, pushing them further and further back. Initially we had merely to maintain the buffer zone because, after the intense fighting in the Green Zone we had experienced on operations like LASTAY KULANG, the OC wanted to let us get our breath back before we launched our next assault.

After about two weeks, 6 Platoon was despatched to FOB Fox for Operation GHARTSI-GHAR, the aim of which was to force the Taliban in the Green Zone to the south and into the jaws of A Company which was waiting for them. The Taliban obviously didn't like the thought of being pushed into this scenario, so decided to attack 5 and 6 Platoons. 7 Platoon stayed back to look after the DC 6 Platoon stayed out there and took some serious casualties through what proved to be a very tough fight. One of the guys, named Giz, was moving forward during a sustained fire fight when an RPG was launched, detonating against a building beside him. The shockwave of the blast snapped his leg and he went down just as a bullet from an AK-47 hit the ground in front of him and then ricocheted up to smash him in the nose. He survived and recovered, and must be one of the luckiest guys I know. 6 Platoon had a horrific time down there, so we felt lucky not to be on the end of that, at least for a while.

In our area, the Taliban wanted to keep hold of Nowzad because it was their staging post from which they launched operations. Their main stronghold was in the north and Musa Qaleh was not that far away, just behind Crocodile Ridge. Due to the ground being so flat, we could observe through our scopes the Taliban in the distance resupplying themselves, but there was not a great deal we could do about it.

One night, I was lying in my pit and Scotty was on stag because we always had to maintain a sentry while we were up on the hill and worked a two hours on, six hours off routine. Suddenly I heard a sudden bang followed by shouts of, 'Medic! Medic! Man down!' I jumped out of bed and was told that Scotty had shot himself accidentally in the hand with his pistol while attempting to clear a stoppage. Luckily, the bullet had not gone through his palm but through the fleshy part underneath his thumb. Although this was very painful, it was a relief that the wound was not more serious. Pete Tointon was on the radio down to DC saying that we had a T3 casualty and giving Scotty's zap number. Our zap numbers were basically our initials, followed by the last four digits of our service numbers, being a quick and secure way of identification over the radio net. I grabbed all of Scotty's details from my day sack and read it out for Pete so he could relay this information back to the DC. I remember Snowy coming out and going mental, shouting, 'What the f... is happening here? Right! I'm f...ing confiscating those f...ing pistols from the lot of you!'

We organised the vehicles to take Scotty back down to the DC, and I volunteered to help take him as he was a fellow sniper. Snowy said, 'Right JC, you're in command of the lead wagon. I will be with Scotty in the other vehicle.' We got our kit and other guys took over on sentry duty as we drove down to the DC. Lance Corporal 'Lamby' Lambell was driving in the darkness as we only had half a moon and no lights. He and I had to try to navigate back to the DC in the darkness as quickly as possible, because Scotty was losing blood and it was a fair distance from the hill to the DC. The problem was there were quite a few different alleyways and roads. If we had taken the wrong one, we could have ended up getting lost and been in serious trouble with a man injured and the Taliban only some 600 metres away. I must admit my heart was thumping big time as we crawled along. I could hear Snowy shouting from the vehicle behind, 'Hurry the f... up! We've got a man down here!' I shouted back, 'Yeah, no problem, sir' before saying to Lamby, 'Have you got any night vis?' He just looked back and said, 'No.' I replied, 'Okay, f...ing floor it mate, just floor it. I'll have to use my Jedi skills,' to which Lamby said, 'Jedi skills? What?' I said, 'Yep, Jedi skills. F...ing floor it mate, just floor it. I'll have to use my Jedi skills.'

We hurtled off down the road. Luckily enough, having only made the trip three times before in daylight, I managed to spot the right alleyway and succeeded in directing Lamby through it. We made our way through alleyways and roads without taking a wrong turn and came bursting into the DC where the gates were already open for us. Scotty was taken into the medical centre there where the medics were ready and waiting for him. They patched him up properly, while Major Aston took a statement. Later, we sat with Scotty and waited for the helicopter which came in at dawn. We got him loaded up and across the helicopter landing site. Thereafter we manned our positions in case of attack and I took hold of my .338 rifle but then realised that I only had the rounds that were in the rifle while the rest of the ammunition for it were in Scotty's kit. I ran across to Pete Tointon and Snowy to tell them, and we grabbed a vehicle and darted down there where we grabbed his kitbag, which contained his L96 rifle and the ammunition for it, as well the rounds for the .338 rifle.

On returning to the hill, we resumed the routine of two hours on sentry and six hours off. I always asked to be woken up half an hour before I was due to go on stag so that I could sort myself out beforehand. I was woken up and made my way over to the 'piss tube' that went deep into the ground. Dressed in boxer shorts and flip flops, I stood there looking out over the incredible landscape of large flat planes of desert, flanked by the beautiful mountain ranges as the sun was slowly coming up and the morning peacefulness surrounded me. All of a sudden, I heard the distinctive whistle of an incoming mortar bomb as it flew over and landed around 400 to 500 metres in front of me. The area of ground in front of me exploded in a maelstrom of dust, dirt, stones and shrapnel which rained down as I ran back up the hill where everyone was shouting, 'In-coming, in-coming! Stand to! Stand to!' Snowy was shouting to everyone to get their helmets and body armour on as I ran back to my kit. As I did so, I lost a flip flop, as another bomb landed only around 200 to 300 metres away. I reached my pit, quickly pulled on some trousers and my body armour, and grabbed my .338 rifle along with my laser rangefinders and ammunition.

When I emerged, Faz was on stag and searching through binoculars in an attempt to locate the enemy position. As I sorted out my rifle and rangefinder, I heard the whistle of another incoming bomb and observed a faint dust cloud right near what we knew to be the Taliban headquarters in the area. I shouted to Faz, 'Firing point seen' and zapped the position with my rangefinder to obtain the distance and bearing while he pinpointed the location on the map, using my figures. He reported this over the radio and immediately afterwards Jacko, our MFC, appeared and took the information from Faz. Lance Corporal Mick Auckland then ran down with a Javelin and command launch unit (CLU). The Javelin is a 'fire and forget' missile, the CLU providing target data to the missile before it is launched and thereafter tracking it to the target until it detonates. Sergeant Major Snow gave the order to fire as soon as Mick shouted out that he had a position lock. Unfortunately, I was standing directly behind the CLU and so received the back blast directly on to my bare feet, which had me dancing around swearing my head off. Mick had set the Javelin to top attack rather than direct, so instead of flying directly towards the target, the missile flew into the air and tracked the target from above. We watched as it went up and up in to the sky until we couldn't see it anymore and then waited until we saw and heard the explosion.

Snowy gave the order for our mortars to open fire and bombard the target area and the anticipated Taliban fall-back positions. They carried out this fire mission so rapidly that they had eight mortar bombs in the air before the first one hit the target; after a few minutes of this, they ceased fire and there was silence. We found out later that we had killed four Taliban and wounded another three.

During our time there, I took part in three or four patrols during which we patrolled to the south of Nowzad up to the edge of the town itself and then pushed in. I remember going up to what was the old hospital which still had the medical posters up with doctors' names and notes written up there. I positioned myself up on the roof along with a few others to provide fire support for some engineers who had been tasked with picking up an old air conditioning unit which they were going to try and repair for us to use in the DC.

We received a few more incoming mortar bombs over the following period, but they were always from a single mortar; on each occasion the Taliban would quickly disappear again, almost as if they were just letting us know they were still there. On one occasion, I was sitting down by the side of the hill chatting away with Faz when the JTAC came over and sat himself down with his radio and kit. He was talking to some American F-15s which were on standby for an American operation that was going on somewhere in the distance. They were doing a circling manoeuvre up high in the night sky and we could hear them as they flew around. The JTAC said that if we looked carefully, we could make out the engines as the glow from the heat was just about visible. The Americans had called in some air support and from seeing a few faint little dots, we could now see glowing triangle shapes as they turned on their afterburners. They were circling around way above us for about five or ten seconds and then they were gone, their afterburners roaring as they headed off towards Musa Qalah.

I spoke to Annie a couple of times through the satellite phone and told her that the hill was haunted and that a few people on sentry duty had heard footsteps behind them, shouted out things like, 'Blimey, you're early!' and then realised that no one was there. This even happened to me a few times, but I still remain sceptical about all that stuff, so it did not really bother me. When I did speak to Annie, she told me that after being with me for a few weeks, she really missed me and felt quite lonely, so I told her to look out at the moon, which she did and told me she could see it. So I said that I was looking at the same moon, so despite the thousands of miles that separated us, in the greater scheme of things, we were both looking at the same thing so we felt close and together. It seemed to help both of us and it was that moment that I had decided to marry her. I remember phoning my brother Ben and saying, 'I have made a decision that when I get back, I am going to propose to Annie and get engaged.' He asked me if I was sure and then congratulated me. He was not enthusiastic about marriage after our parents divorced, but did support me and was genuinely happy for me.

Teddy was now back from R & R, but had deployed directly to Kajaki as that was where we would carry out the final phase of our operational tour. C Company was already there and starting on MOGs to ensure the Taliban did not re-infiltrate Sangin, while we would be making sure that Kajaki was safe and not infiltrated by the Taliban from our side. On 20 July, we moved out of Nowzad and headed for Kajaki.

CHAPTER 15

Kajaki I

W e were picked up by Chinook helicopters that brought in a few guys from C Company to help man our positions in Nowzad. Before leaving, I saw Tom and Sergeant Head from the Sniper Platoon and showed them ANP Hill before we left, using the opportunity to obtain information from them about the Kajaki area. They told us about one village called Mazdurak which had seen some really quite serious action during which a lot of bombs were dropped, and warned us to expect an interesting time if we were deployed there. We also learnt that Kajaki was split between two regions to the north and south; to the south lay an area similar to the Green Zone which we knew so well. The main village to the south was called Kajaki Sofla, a name we recognized from the briefings we had already been given on the area.

As we approached Kajaki, we could see the huge reservoir with its massive expanse of deep blue water against the orangey brown colour of the ground. The terrain was very mountainous, as was generally the case on the border between Helmand and Pakistan to the far south of the province. We flew in and out of a series of canyons and ravines as we approached the big blue reservoir, the pilot banking the aircraft sharply and then sweeping low as we went along. A Chinook had been bought down in this area during a previous tour, so he was ensuring that we did not share the same fate.

As we flew over the reservoir, the RAF loadmaster test fired the aircraft's weapons, firing down into the water. There was a 7.62mm machine gun on the back of the ramp and a multi-barrelled chain gun on the side of the helicopter. After that came the familiar pat on the shoulder and two fingers were held up signifying two minutes to land. As soon as the Chinook touched down, we jumped out and ran under the blades away from the helicopter, passing a few guys from C Company heading in the opposite direction to embark on the aircraft. After only around twenty or thirty seconds the Chinook was gone and out of sight, while we sat and waited to be ferried into Forward Operating Base Zeebrugge. Shortly afterwards, we were picked up by a Pinzgauer vehicle and driven past the dam, which we were there to defend, and then down a very steep valley with the Helmand River below us.

Having settled into the base and talking to some of the guys about the area, we learned that that the surrounding area had three observation posts (OPs) positioned on the four main peaks of the mountainous terrain known as Athens, Normandy, Sparrow-Hawk East and Sparrow-Hawk West. When the Marines first arrived, one of their main tasks had been to clear the Taliban from these locations as they had already taken control of Athens and Sparrow-Hawk East. The enemy had the advantage of knowing every inch of the area and were able to navigate the minefield on the way to the top and then once there, bring fire down on the camp below. The Marines gained control of the area and then manned it fully. On going up there ourselves, we realised what a difficult place to fight it was, being steep and rocky with an old Russian anti-personnel minefield on top. The metre-wide track that led to and from all the OPs had been cleared as a safe route but even this was not brilliantly marked out as all we could see was a rough footpath where the ground was slightly bare.

The three OPs had excellent views of the whole area and we could see literally everything, including all the little villages and how Kajaki was split from north to south, with the north having almost no greenery at all but large numbers of wadis, the main one of which we called the A1 Wadi. C Company had managed to push the Taliban back through towards the north and having the four OPs now meant that we knew immediately when the Taliban encroached into our area. As a result, FOB Zeebrugge was very safe and hardly ever attacked.

To the South, there was Olya village and then Sofla which was far more of a Green Zone with grass, trees and densely populated compounds. We could see where the Taliban headquarters was located, around a mile away from the OPs. They had a lot of women and children there, so we could not engage the headquarters itself; when we did engage them, we observed that they always retreated back into this area.

C Company had carried out larger scale pre-planned operations during its time up there but was now conducting MOGs in the area to the north east of Sangin. A and C Companies were now giving the Taliban a difficult time, squeezing them hard in the Jucelay and Putay area. The Taliban were determined to keep Sangin under control because it was a pivotal area for them.

Whenever the opportunity arose, we used to take spare vehicles down to the reservoir to swim in its ice cold water, a blissful relief from the intense heat of July and August when the daytime temperature was in the mid-fifties. Although the local Afghan police were there to make sure it was safe, we still needed to be alert and very vigilant with our vehicles ready to move at a moment's notice.

All too soon the time came for us to return to the arduous and dangerous business of going out on patrol. There was a small group of C Company who had remained to give us a full hand-over brief, Robbo from the Sniper Platoon coming out with us on one of our initial patrols. These were primarily for us to familiarise ourselves properly with the ground out there and so we took the WMIKs. We soon learned that the situation in this area was far more predictable and we could almost plan from a timing perspective how things would play out. The fighting was at a far slower pace than we had experienced already. We carried out some patrols in the early hours of the morning, which were more probing than anything else, but we made sure they were varied in timing and areas. We patrolled more frequently to the north, mainly because there was a greater area to cover than in the south, which was squashed between Sofla, the Helmand River and the high mountain range. There was really only one route in the south from which the Taliban could approach and that was covered by the Afghan police and Afghan National Army. Also the OPs could view the whole area and, if they observed the Taliban in any numbers, could attack with Javelin missiles and GPMGs from above.

A typical day began at 3.00 am, with us carrying out radio checks and other procedures before moving out at around 4.00 am in the darkness when it was still cool. We would reach our lying up position (LUP), clear the area and then by around 9.00 or 10.00 am begin falling back. We would generally arrive at FOB Zeebrugge by around 11.00 in time for breakfast or brunch. We would go to our rooms in the main building to clean weapons and see Company Sergeant Major Newton to replenish our ammunition. We could also wash after our patrols because water was pumped up from the river to the base so we could have showers. There was unlimited untreated water for washing and a butt of clean drinking water.

At around 5.00 pm we would receive our orders and then I would go on the text link to contact home, followed by grabbing some food which in this place was better than normal. When we were not on patrol and had some down time, we could relax in front of the television. As I was normally up in the early hours, I used to get to bed at around 10.00 pm after the normal routine of packing and preparing my kit for the following day.

It was at that point that B Company had a new OC, Major Tony Borgnis, who arrived to take over from Major Aston. I remember the first time I met him when he walked over and said, 'Hello, James. How are you?' I thought, 'How do you know my name? You are the new OC and I don't know if this is a good or a bad thing.' We all wondered what it would be like working under a new OC as we in the FSG had all grown used to working for Major Mick Aston over the last four months of the tour. Although, like all good commanders, he kept a boundary between the men and himself, he was hands-on and got involved with the men and was really down to earth. Little things like asking how you were. You could tell he was genuine about this, a good guy and a good commander.

On patrol, I would carry my normal six litres of water, my L96 rifle, 200 rounds of ammunition, laser range finders, my 9mm pistol with two spare magazines, two HE grenades, two phosphorus grenades, a trauma kit consisting of one syrette of morphine, two first field dressings (FFDs) and a tourniquet. I didn't have to carry a radio any more as Major Borgnis wanted to have as many snipers on the ground as possible. This meant that Teddy and I split up and would rely on the radios of whoever we were ordered to accompany. Sometimes we would work with the FSG, on other occasions we would be placed with the rifle platoons.

The first proper patrol we conducted on this leg of the tour was up in a place called Shrine Hill, where there was a small shrine dug into the hill. On this occasion we had mine detectors bought up to us and, as we patrolled in the darkness, the guys were sweeping the track in front of them as they slowly walked up, all spread-out and looking down over Masdurak. We could see B Company down below us beginning to go through and get a decent look at the area, mainly reconnaissance for the commanders who wanted to obtain a good picture idea of the ground ahead. The first building was almost like a scene out of the film *Stalingrad*. It was just reduced to rubble and I recalled that Tom had been right when he had said that a lot of ordinance had been dropped on the area.

Meanwhile, Teddy and I were in one of the WMIKs up on the hill and we set about positioning a 'gun line' up there on the top. We had three GPMGs on sustained fire (SF) mounts on tripods that provided greater accuracy over longer ranges. I was on one of them, Strikey was on another and Gill manned the one in the middle. While we had been setting up, the guys from B Company pushed around below and began to clear one of the villages across the wadi. The three of us laid down SF down from the hill across the wadi and then into the village – always in front of the guys as they pushed through. This proved to be successful and we managed to clear the village successfully with no casualties. As we were clearing the village, we had some air cover from some F-15s. One aircraft screamed down low to the ground in a show of force which was very impressive, before banking upwards and throwing off flares all over the place.

On another occasion, I was patrolling with 6 Platoon and clearing two villages in the early hours of the morning. It was initially a pretty standard operation as we went in, continually upscaling and downscaling from code red to code green and then amber code while moving through. Soon we began to come under some pretty heavy fire from the north where there was a large area of open ground in front of us, forming a gap between the two villages. Jay, who had taught me on my sniper cadre and was now in B Company, asked for my laser rangefinders, so I passed them up to him on the roof. He could see some of the Taliban moving around and, having been a sniper for many years, he began firing at them. I then slung my L96, pulled my pistol out, found the platoon sergeant and told him that I would be his runner as Jay was up there using my rangefinders and there was no room for anyone else up on the roof. He told me to go and collect 51mm bombs for the mortar men.

As I busily collected the bombs, the mortar man was firing away with what he already had. He was running low by the time I arrived with a fresh supply. Up to this point he had been firing and loading the mortar on his own, which is tough because you need two hands to operate the mortar. The noise of the mortar firing was incredibly loud, but he was unable to stick his fingers in his ears and fire at the same time. As a result, the poor bloke's ears were ringing like mad while Sergeant Browning was shouting out ranges and where he wanted the bombs. I was relaying the information, but the mortar man was simply looking at me shouting, 'What?' I was reduced to mouthing what I was saying in an exaggerated fashion, whilst using hand signals, so it was like talking to a foreigner, 'High angle, 200 metres on that line', all done with hand signals and mouthing the words. He was saying, 'What? Eh?'

In the end I resorted to using my notebook and wrote the instructions in it, He read them and shouted at the top of his voice, 'OK, but what line?' I relayed his question to Sergeant Browning who came over and showed me, and I used my day sack for the mortar man to follow this line. As I tapped the poor bloke on the shoulder and put my thumbs up mouthing, 'Fire now, fire now', he winced as the next onslaught on his ear drums was about to come and fired. My fingers were in my ears but, as I took them out, I could hear his low moaning of, 'Ahhh!' A few moments later, the call again came over for us to fire another bomb but to add fifty metres, so I wrote on my note pad, 'Add fifty.' He lined the mortar up again, winced and fired while shouting, 'Ow! You f...ing bastard!' while wincing in pain. I could not help but laugh.

At this point, I wanted to be back in the action, so went back to where Jay was still busy firing away up on the roof. He shouted down, 'Got any more magazines, mate?' I threw them up to him as he tossed down some empty magazines, which I began to reload. As I did so, I called up and asked, 'Have you got anyone yet?' He told me that he was trying to take out one guy in particular; at that moment, there was a loud crack and a bullet smashed into the side of the wall to the right of where he was lying. The path of the round had clearly only just missed him so crawled back on his belly and eventually dropped down off the roof, explaining that there was an enemy sniper out there who he was trying to locate. We worked out that the round had come from the left, so I took my rifle and rangefinders and moved round to the side of the building. I was trying to see over the open ground and observed one or two buildings in the distance.

I could not see any movement, so lined up my rangefinders, zapped the distance and then checked the roofs and looked into the windows of each building. I then moved up to an archway and on to a bit of a rise from where I looked across to one of a number of water butts on top of a building where someone indicated that they were sure a man was positioned. I put a few rounds to either side of this to see if I could produce some movement, but nothing happened. There was a wall behind which the Taliban were moving and every now and then we would see an AK-47 pop up and fire over, but it was pretty much firing blind. The enemy sniper was still out there and I wanted to find him, so kept looking towards the left hand side. Even though he clearly was not the best of shots, or he would have hit Jay, he obviously could move really well and was proving difficult to locate. Another crack rang out, indicating he was still there. Eventually the call came for us to pull out of there and, as we were doing this, we came across a tunnel. We had grenades at the ready to throw down it while a sapper rigged up a bar mine to blow the tunnel which collapsed at our end, so preventing the Taliban from using it and coming up behind us as we pulled back.

On the next patrol, we were tasked with clearing the village of Shomali Gulbah. It was a similar story, with me up on to a roof alongside 7 Platoon with Josh Lee and Private 'Ronnie' Barker. The three of us were moving in and around of these domes that were like giant Smarties tubes cut in half and laid on top of the roof, about a metre or so high. There was a row of trees in front of us, so I was trying to position myself to lay fire down into this area, because we could see the flashes of the weapons as the Taliban fired.

At that point, I heard the distinctive sound of that enemy sniper rifle once more. I knew it was being fired from quite some distance this time, as the length of the pause between the crack of the bullet passing to my left and the thump of the noise of the weapon being fired gave this away. Ronnie and I thought that the sniper's tactics were that, once the main body of Taliban guys engaged us and bogged us down, he would move out to the open area to our left and fire from there. I manoeuvred myself around even more to the left, with Ronnie joining me to help look for the sniper, while Josh Lee concentrated on the buildings in front of us. I gave Ronnie my rangefinders so he could have a good look while I prepared my L96. I looked through the scope and focused on a building in the distance to use as my average range, which I set at 400 metres; if anything came up within that range, I would have to aim lower.

As I set myself up, Ronnie and I were spotted by the sniper. There was a sudden crack as a round whizzed past my face; it was so close I could feel the wind from it, making me jolt my head backwards. Ronnie hit the deck and we both had our bellies on the floor as we looked at each other thinking, 'F..., that was close!' We shouted for supporting fire and the calls went out, 'Rapid Fire! Rapid Fire!' to which Private Thrumble responded with his GPMG. The other machine gunners began to lay down fire too, along with Josh Lee. Meanwhile, we crawled off that roof as fast as we could. That was another close call and I remembered what Robbo had said previously about a sniper popping up before and that they had dug out one of the rounds that had embedded itself in to the wall. It was one of the rare times the enemy used a .50 calibre round. The rumours circulated that the sniper might have been a Chechyen because the Taliban don't normally have access to that kind of kit. If the Taliban were going to use any kind of sniper rifle against us, it would more than likely be a Dragunov which fires a 7.62mm calibre round and not a .50.

On another occasion, we were pushing up towards Masdurak at night, just to see if we could catch anyone out moving around in the dark. We had been out for a good two or three hours and had moved back towards the southern side of Shrine Hill. There was a relatively prominent dusty road which ran from east to west and we were moving along this road towards the west of Shrine Hill. Suddenly the OP's voice came over the radio and said, 'Stop! Stop, stop! There are enemy behind you.' These were unidentified and were possibly Taliban following us up the road. It appeared that they were halting whenever we went firm, this being an indication they were definitely following and watching us.

We moved swiftly off the track and into a deep crater, caused by an exploding bomb, where we positioned ourselves and observed back towards the east. There were two platoons out on patrol that night, so it was decided that one of the platoons should take up position within the few compounds that ran adjacent to the road on the southern side while we remained in the crater. Teddy and I were working together on this patrol and I had my SA80 rifle fitted with a CWS and my radio, while Teddy had his .338 rifle equipped with night optics. We waited and watched in the darkness.

The commander of 7 Platoon, Lieutenant Seal-Coon, pointed out Shrine Hill to our left and a crumbling ruin just to our rear and said, 'Do you want to get up there with Teddy while we cover you from down here?.' We would be able to see further from up high so we gathered ourselves to get up there. I asked the boss if I could borrow a VIPIR thermal imaging sight, so I would be able to see the same images as the guys who had initially radioed the information and he agreed. The sight can be attached to the SA80 rifle and you can set it to show heat sources in white or in black; in white, all the terrain and rocks around us would show up in black, but anything hot like bodies, or car exhaust pipes for example would show up in white with everything else being various shades of grey. It really does give one a good image in the dark, but you have the option to change this around and have the heat sources showing up in black with the cold items in white and the other shades of grey. I always preferred white hot as previously I had used the larger and bulkier 'Sophie' unit which was similar to a pair of binoculars.

The guy from whom I borrowed the VIPIR had not zeroed the sight to his SA80 as he was using it in the kind of hand-held role instead. Anyway, I took it, briefed Teddy on what we were going to do and we began making our way to the ruin. As we did so, we received a running commentary on the guys following us. They had not moved since our patrol had halted and moved off the track, so as Teddy and I moved towards the ruins, we kept very low to ensure they could not see us.

We scrambled up through the ruin on our hands and knees, turning right at the back of the building and taking a narrow trail towards the higher ground that lay to the rear from which we would able to look down on the entire area. We moved very slowly and carefully as we did not want to dislodge any loose debris or the odd boulder and give away our position. When we arrived at a point where we felt comfortable, Teddy positioned himself three metres to the right of me. We communicated by whispering into our respective PRRs, rather than trying to talk normally. Teddy sorted himself out but could not see anything through his night vision kit. I took out my rangefinders and tried to give him the ranges he needed. Despite only just being able to make out the buildings around 500 to 600 metres away, I managed to zap them and record the ranges. I called the OPs on the radio and they confirmed that they could see us. I then asked if they could tell me roughly how far we were from the enemy, so I could narrow down the range and get them in my sights. They told us that the Taliban were closer to us than the buildings I had zapped and were actually only around 300 or 400 metres away. Teddy set his rifle's scope to 300, took off his safety catch and waited for any kind of movement.

I was using the VIPIR, but still could not see anything of interest. I had been told that the enemy were now moving south towards the track. This gave me a good point of reference, so I kept observing and then suddenly could just see them and now had them in my sights. There were two figures who appeared to me were crawling rather than walking. Teddy said that they looked more like dogs. I agreed and radioed the OP which was convinced they were real people and not dogs; at the same time I also heard from the patrol commander who was asking me what we could see. I could only say what I saw and said that I was 95% sure it was two dogs. The OP was asking if I was sure and I responded by saying that I was a lot closer to the heat signatures and could say that I was almost 100% sure they were dogs as they were moving too fast. Surprise, surprise, shortly afterwards I saw two wagging tails as they approached us and realised they were our platoon's two adopted dogs, Tangye and Charlie, who had clearly followed our scent. The patrol continued heading back to base without further incident.

A few days later we were patrolling up near Masdurak and this time I had been placed with Corporal Si Thorn's section in 5 Platoon. We made our way up through the broken buildings and had been around Masdurak so many times now that we pretty much knew what to expect. We did not bother throwing in grenades because by this stage we had managed to increase the buffer zone between us and the Taliban whom we had pushed back beyond Masdurak and as far away from the dam as possible. As a result, it had become more like a routine as we swept through, patrolling these areas with everyone knowing each alleyway and doorway and generally knowing exactly what to do. We moved through swiftly, remaining vigilant all the time. We moved through to the other side of Masdurak. On this occasion we were deployed as flank protection on the westerly side as the main body went through. The guys we were covering were going in to clear a place called Chinah. Further to the right hand side we had the WMIKs and the gun line up on what we called Essex Hill, looking down into a village called Risaji. We were all in our positions and my guys readied themselves on the western flank as B Company, which was the main group, moved in.

Meanwhile, we had received intelligence that a couple of Taliban sentries had been cut off from the main group. They had been out there resting up and had fallen asleep as we had moved into our positions under the cover of night and cut them off. We were to hunt them down.

We could hear the small arms fire starting and the mortars joining in off to the right as the main group went in. Si Thorn and I remained in position, chatting away to kill time while listening to the radio reports of a heavy engagement. As we did so, we saw some civilians that we did not want to come too close so we decided that a couple of shots would serve as a warning to keep them out of the way. There was a telegraph pole about 600 metres away in the same area and Si bet me ten US dollars that I could not hit it with one shot. I readied myself for our little challenge and took my shot. Both of us hearing the ping as my bullet hit the pole. Laughing, I claimed my ten dollars as Si then challenged me to hit the telegraph wire. I gave it a go but missed. Someone, meanwhile, had heard my shots and radioed in asking if we were okay, which, of course, we were. In any event, the shots had the required effect on the civvies who legged it safely out of danger.

My target practice also produced another unexpected result. I had sited myself back up on one of the rooftops so I could carry on observing some buildings a few hundred metres away. I had dialled the range of 200 metres into the scope on my rifle and began looking through it into each window and door, searching for any movement. As I observed an open doorway, it was suddenly filled by a Taliban sentry wearing a green robe, black waistcoat and the tell-tale black turban, with an AK-47 in his hands and a couple of RPG rounds standing up over his shoulder. I already had my safety catch off and so lined him up and squeezed the trigger. He dropped immediately, the impact of the bullet pushing him back through the doorway. We followed the shot up by firing a couple of 40mm grenades from a UGL into the doorway in case he was not alone. We then fired two more through the windows to make absolutely sure. We then radioed in and said, 'We have spotted an enemy sentry and have engaged with one confirmed dead with possibly more, stand by.' We then fired more 40mm grenades into the building for around another thirty seconds before asking for permission to go down there and check the buildings.

This was refused and we were told to remain in position. We stayed there without further incident and then eventually moved back, continuing to give flanking cover to B Company after the operation had been successfully carried out.

On another occasion we were on patrol again out to the north of Kajaki, but this time Teddy and I rode in the back of one of the WMIKs. We needed to get up on to Essex Ridge to offer sniper cover from there as we had been receiving a considerable amount of fire from the Taliban in the village of Risaji. A couple of shell scrapes had already been dug on the ridge by either C Company or the Marines before them, so they could position a gun line there for the GPMGs. We had Jay with us and were more than happy to have him along to give us a hand. Behind the ridge were the WMIKs so that we could use the extra fire support of the .50 heavy machine mounted on the back of them. They would be ready and able to reverse up to the ridgeline just behind us to fire over our heads and the crest of the hill down into Risaji if we needed them to do so. I positioned myself in one of the shell scrapes, while Teddy and Jay took the other further 40 or 50 metres away to my right.

Our guys went in with supporting mortar fire using a mixture of HE and smoke bombs. As we looked down into Risaji, we dialled in the range of the nearest buildings which lay around 500 metres away. All of a sudden, we came under heavy fire from an RPD, a belt-fed 7.62mm calibre machine gun which equates roughly to our own GPMG. We all hit the floor but after a few seconds I realised the fire was concentrating to my right, with bullets impacting and ricocheting in and around Teddy's and Jay's shell scrape. I put my head above the parapet and tried to look for the enemy firing position and could just make out the tell-tale small puffs of dust coming from a building around 400 metres away. There were two compounds with several trees around them and a long wall separating the two buildings by around 60 or 70 metres. I fired two rounds into the where the dust was coming from, my aim being to warn them, through the distinctive crack and thump sound of my L96 rifle, that they were under fire from a sniper.

My ploy worked as the firing stopped after my second shot. I was yelling, 'Teddy, Teddy! Are you okay?' All of a sudden, I saw a thumb briefly appear from the shell scrape and equally swiftly vanish again, which made me crack up laughing. Jay shouted out, 'Did you see where it came from?' To which I replied, 'Yeah, building to the right, building to the right! About 400 metres away. I put a few rounds in.'

Teddy and Jay then peered over the rim of their shell and, as they did so, I came under fire. The Taliban had shifted position and now it was my turn. I could hear the whistle and hiss of bullets and slammed myself on to the floor of my shell scrape as they flew literally inches from my head. I adopted the foetal position with my rifle next to me as bullets thudded into the ground and ricocheted all over the place. All I could do was curl up and make myself as small as possible while screaming, 'F...ing hell! F...ing hell!' at the top of my lungs. Every time I tried to breathe in, I choked on the dust thrown up by the bullets all around me and I could only see dust and shards of stones. Things were pinging off my helmet and body armour and my body clenched and tightened up every time something hit me. Although it only lasted for around ten seconds, it seemed to last for hours and hours.

Like I had before, Teddy and Jay had spotted the Taliban position and fired a handful of rounds, which forced the enemy to cease fire. The role reversal continued as they then called out to me, 'JC, JC! Are you all right?.' I raised my trembling, shaking thumb and quickly brought it back down, hearing them hear them both laughing as I did so. I cracked up myself, as though someone had told me the funniest joke ever. Eventually, I succeeded in forcing my trembling hands to put a cigarette in my mouth and light it. It took all of my inner strength to pull myself back up and put my head back over the parapet as a potential target once more.

By this time the WMIKs had reversed up the hill and were now laying down fire over our heads and down into the area with their .50 heavy machine guns. This took the pressure off us, so we could start observing and firing at likely targets. After around two or three more hours, we clambered out of our respective shell scrapes and into the back of the WMIKs. I can't speak for the others, but I certainly went back to FOB Zeebrugge with slightly wobbly legs that day.

CHAPTER 16

Kajaki II

We had to patrol to the south as well as the north, and on this occasion I went south with Sergeant Chris Caneper of 5 Platoon with whom I had worked previously. We were pushing the Taliban back towards their headquarters in the south, which we had already identified, and were to the West of the 611 road which ran from Kajaki all the way down into the Sangin Valley. We were in the WMIKs and Pinzgauer vehicles, which took us all the way down to the Afghan police checkpoint situated where the Helmand River turns sharply at a 90 degree angle southwards. There they dropped us off.

The Green Zone was between the Helmand River and the 611 road and we were pushing down on the eastern side of the 611. To the rear of us were two WMIKs deployed up on the ridgeline and behind them were the OPs Sparrow-Hawks East and West which could provide overhead supporting fire with their .50 heavy machine guns and Javelin missiles if necessary. We also had air cover as we pushed further south, passing by ruined buildings, in area which had witnessed so much fighting over the years. We needed to keep parallel with B Company as it was engaged in a heavy contact, so we were slowing up as we made our way through alleyways and buildings while ensuring that B Company was not flanked from our side. To our left was rocky mountainous ground that had been mined during the Russian occupation but, after years of movement in the ground, known as 'mine migration', there was no way of knowing the exact location of the mines so we had to tread with great care.

KAJAKI II

I positioned myself on a rooftop with quite a high wall that ran from my left to right, while Sergeant Caneper and a group of four guys were the other side of the wall on another rooftop overlooking a large courtyard area. We were giving each other mutual support and covering fire as we went through the area. At that point we spotted a group of civilians, coming down the hillside to our left, who stopped and sat down when they saw us. I observed them through my scope but could not see any weapons. OP Sparrow-Hawk had also spotted them and was keeping an eye on them as they seemed to have appeared from nowhere.

There were sixteen of us trying to create this buffer zone as the lads from B Company were fighting nearby. We could not see them, but could hear the contact as it continued. OP Sparrow-Hawk then informed us that a group of Taliban was moving almost directly towards us, not knowing we were there. After a few minutes we could hear the distinctive sound of men shouting in Pashto approaching us. We were near a road with alleyways and buildings leading off in all directions, and trees randomly dotted around the area. The adrenaline was pumping through me and it was quite scary knowing that these guys were literally on the other side of this area and could pop out at anytime. Suddenly I saw some of them running down an alleyway. One of them, wearing a white robe with a black waistcoat and armed with an AK-47, took what he thought was cover and spun round firing back in to the Green Zone. I lined him up in my sights and, at a range of 300 or 400 metres away, fired one shot and killed him.

Alerted to our presence by my shot, the other fighters brought heavy fire to bear on us. We returned it, with Robbie McCall next to me suddenly standing up and launching an AT-4 which is an 84mm anti-tank rocket launched from an expendable launcher that is discarded after use. It makes a massive noise when launched and so, with ringing ears, I spun around and called him a prick for not warning me. He merely grinned as he threw down the empty launcher tube and carried on firing with his SA80. The firing from the Taliban died down considerably after the rocket hit a nearby building where some of them were located. I reckon it killed about four or five of them at least.

Shortly afterwards, we climbed off the rooftops as by then B Company had pushed as far as it could go, having reached its limit of exploitation (LOE), the point beyond which they were not permitted to advance. We moved back, keeping level with B Company until we reached the pick-up point where we were ferried back to base in the vehicles.

On another patrol to the south, I was commanding one of the WMIKS and had Faz as my driver and Reedy on the .50 heavy machine gun up on the top mount. There were only about three places where we could position the vehicles from which to give proper support. Even though we varied our routines, the Taliban still had a 33% chance of getting it right and being there to meet us. We normally had around ten minutes of firing before we would begin to receive returning fire and RPGs launched at us. I normally spent most of my time running around and clambering on to roofs, so driving in a WMIK was much easier. WMIKS are not fitted with any armour other than ballistic matting. We were out in the open, providing an unprotected target for the Taliban.

B Company was going in down below us. I had a GPMG mounted in front of me and together with another WMIK began to provide supporting fire. We were deployed on a ridgeline and were beginning to come under heavy fire, with RPGs literally whizzing just over our heads, one impacting on a building right next to us and showering us with debris and shrapnel. In spite of this we continued to provide support, while also launching a few Javelin missiles. This continued for about three hours until B Company reached its LOE, at which point we began withdrawing.

Back on my normal patrols and with sniper rifle in hand, I joined Sergeant Caneper once more for our last patrol in the south. B Company went in with 5 Platoon taking the supporting positions to the left, protecting the flank and moving forward in parallel. This time it was similar to patrols in Masdurak in the sense that we had information that there were no large pockets of Taliban waiting for us. We patrolled through the various buildings and alleyways, without using grenades but still sweeping through on a green code. I was behind one of the guys as we walked near a building opposite Kajaki

KAJAKI II

Sofla and watched as another nearby suddenly froze and held up his hand. I asked him what was wrong and he said, 'Pressure plate. I think I can see a pressure plate.' A pressure plate is a homemade device which typically uses a piece of wood about the size of a cricket bat, with something similar to a saw blade on top along with two nails underneath, poking out of the wood towards the saw blade. There is an electric current connected to the nails, so when you stand on the saw blade, it flexes and touches the two nails, completing the circuit and detonating a mine or improvised explosive device (IED) buried nearby.

We reported the find so that the EOD team could come down and take a look but, at the time, the Taliban were kicking off big style with B Company in the Green Zone. We had to work fast because we realised that we weren't going to get the EOD team and we needed to try to identify the type of device. The guy in front of me got down on his hands and knees and began to sweep the ground on the other side of the pressure plate, eventually locating the command wire that led to an anti-tank mine buried only around a centimetre from the surface. You can imagine the damage this would have done, bearing in mind that it was designed to blow up a tank. I recorded the grid reference on my hand-held GPS device and decided to pull out of there, but just as we began to move down an alleyway we came under heavy fire from the front and right. We began to fire back but saw that B Company was beginning to pull back, so we did the same as we did not want to be left swinging in the breeze.

The Taliban had obviously anticipated the direction from which we would approach, hence the mine. B Company was now coming up against some very stiff resistance. At the same time, we heard the crack of supporting fire from the OP over our heads. We jumped over walls, ran through buildings and bolted through alleyways, laying fire down as we went and covering each other all the time as we moved. We reached a high wall, probably as high as seven or eight feet, and could hear the Taliban shouting to each other as they closed in on us. When they were really close, three of our guys threw grenades over the wall simultaneously. There were three explosions followed by screams of pain so we knew we hit some of them, but were not keen on hanging around to find out how many so made ourselves scarce as quickly as possible. We were still under heavy fire from what appeared to be everywhere, including windows and doorways, as we went. It was a pretty hairy moment but somehow we managed to escape without anyone being killed or seriously injured, so all in all it was a successful, if scary, patrol.

We had seen some real action in both the north and south of the area, but now headed to the far north, a number of miles further than we had operated previously. On deploying, we moved up a wadi and saw a compound of four buildings, with one in each corner. To the left there was a high hill and in the distance we could see around five or six more compounds strung out one after the other in a straight line going away from us. To the right there was another high feature and beyond the buildings was another bit of the Green Zone.

We moved up to the north-east of these compounds and once again I was with Sergeant Caneper and 5 Platoon. We were to provide fire support for 6 Platoon which was going to carry out a pincer movement to the right. With the WMIKS in support, the platoon pushed right around us over the open ground and then across the bottom of the high feature to the right-hand side, eventually breaking into the compounds leading away from us. Just to the left of these was another large one surrounded by trees where I spotted some men digging as our guys crossed the open ground. I could see no weapons but reported it to Sergeant Caneper who also had a look. I told him that I was keeping a close eye on them and he responded by saying that if I spotted anything or any weapons, I should engage them first and then tell him.

I zapped the building with my rangefinders and set my scope to the distance of the compound, which was around 600 metres away. As soon as our guys began to fire and break into the compounds, the Afghans dropped their tools and ran into the house. This once again was not necessarily suspicious as they looked like farmers who simply wanted to get the hell out of the way of any trouble, but I kept my eyes on the house while 6 Platoon finished clearing the compounds before withdrawing over the open ground under cover of the WMIKS.

KAJAKI II

All of a sudden I saw tell-tale puffs of smoke as the Afghans in the building I was watching began firing at 6 Platoon, so I scanned the windows and doors waiting for them to show themselves. I eventually saw one of them, wearing a black turban and dark robes, firing through a window. I lined up the shot, held my breath and fired, watching as he threw his arms up in the air and fell backwards. 6 Platoon took cover from the open ground and it was now our turn to begin extraction. Sergeant Caneper and I would obviously be the last people to come off the roof as he was in charge and I was the sniper who could see furthest. He jumped down and, as I began to follow, I heard the crack of a sniper round and threw myself flat. The enemy sniper had obviously been watching us but fortunately had missed. I crawled to the edge of the roof and handed down my L96 rifle. I had to manoeuvre over this ledge but clearly was not keen on showing my head again, so began sliding down the ladder head first. About halfway down, my hands slipped and I fell, landing like a bag of spuds on the ground. It did hurt a bit and I looked ridiculous, but pissed myself laughing as did Sergeant Caneper who gave me a hand-up before I checked the gash on my hand and other bumps and bruises. The only thing we could do now with a sniper operating in the area was literally to run the four miles back to base, which is exhausting in such heat but the thought of a bullet between the eyes kept us going.

On 25 July, Teddy had heard some news which was really devastating. He had been in the Ops room, waiting to use the satellite phone to call home, and had been told that Operation MINIMISE, the procedure put into force when someone had been killed in action, had been activated. The reason for the name MINIMISE was because all communication with the world outside had to cease. You are not allowed to telephone, send a text, email or communicate in any way with the outside world. This is to ensure that the family of the dead soldier hear the news first from the Ministry of Defence and not from the media.

We obviously wanted to find out what had happened, but it was all very sketchy. That evening, we could only listen to the radio in the Ops room for any further news. We eventually learned that there had been an IED incident involving one of our convoys within the FOB Inkerman area, near Putay and Jucelay.

The worrying aspect was that there were two confirmed T1 casualties, but that was all we knew. Teddy took copies of the ZAP numbers, which were designed to identify anyone quickly over the radio as we were not permitted to mention anyone's names for obvious security reasons. As I have mentioned before, a ZAP number consisted of your first and last name initials, followed by the last four numbers of your regimental number. Older soldiers still referred to it as your NI PIN (Northern Ireland Personal Identification Number). Teddy took down these numbers and we immediately had a sense of dread as we saw the letters AH and four numbers. We feared that something had happened to Alex as he was one of our snipers within the area, and his surname was Hawkins.

I had a list of all the ZAP numbers because of all of the kit issued to individuals back in the UK. We were frantic to discover if this was our comrade and friend – in particular, the person I had spent so long bunked with in the same room and who was almost like a brother to me. We were trying not to fear the worst, hoping that he had just broken something and required morphine. This would explain why he had been a T1, because requirement for morphine automatically classifies you as a T1 casualty as it just knocks you out and you need to be carried. We prayed to everything we held dear that this was the case.

I went rooting through my kit and finally found the list. Our worst fears were realised – it was of course Alex, and so we now knew he was a T1 casualty. It was so frustrating as we spent the whole day, with time dragging out as far as you could imagine, just waiting for news and there was nothing we could do. I slept inside the building that night as we had no patrols to do and eventually fell asleep.

On the following morning, I awoke with Teddy leaning over me and gently shaking me by my shoulder. I will always remember his long, pale face staring down at me, spelling bad news. I sat up and the feeling of dread deepened as he then handed me a cigarette and lighter. As I lit the cigarette, he just said it, 'Alex has died, mate.'

I honestly did not know what to say, so just there looking up at Teddy's face and feeling as though the wind had been knocked out of me, I was totally lost for words. I will never know how long I remained silent, looking up at Teddy and into space, but it felt around 15 minutes as the enormity of what had happened slowly sank in and the reality that my true friend had died took hold. It is a strange feeling when this happens and it is very difficult to describe. It is not the same as an elderly relative that you love passing away, because Alex was a person who was not only young and in his prime, but also someone with whom I had formed a different kind of bond. You just do not form bonds like that in normal life because you have not gone through the trials and tests of conflict that bring such closeness. I felt devastated, as though my own brother had died.

It turned out that what had happened was that Alex was on a vehicle patrol on which he was in command of a Vector, the brand new version of the Pinzgauer with better armour. IEDs were actually fairly rare at the time, even though they are now commonplace because the Taliban have changed tactics after finding themselves unable to beat the British Army in toe–to–toe combat. The Taliban had worked out how to attack the new, heavier armoured vehicles by placing the IEDs at an angle in the ground instead of laying them straight up against the vehicle.

If you put too much armour on a vehicle and then try and take a corner at 30 or 40 mph, there is a real danger that you will just roll it so you have to slow down. In this case, as the convoy rounded a corner and slowed down, the vehicle in front then sped up considerably and increased the gap between it and Alex's vehicle behind. Alex naturally attempted to catch up but, in doing so, created another problem. It is hard enough to spot an IED at normal pace, and almost impossible to do so at high speed. Alex's vehicle hit one with devastating results.

One of the first on the scene was Kingy, also a member of the Sniper Platoon. One of the other guys from the vehicle, Pat, who was part of FSG, was conscious and shouting and screaming in pain. The first guys to arrive on the scene obviously left him initially as he was responsive, concentrating their efforts on the unresponsive one who was Alex. Their reasons for doing so are pretty clear as if you cannot shout for help, you are likely in a bad way and in need of help urgently. Three or four of the guys tried to tend to his wounds and save his life, while a helicopter was scrambled from Camp Bastion.

The medical team at Bastion tried everything they could but tragically failed to save Alex's life. He was T1 from the outset, but you always cling on to hope in these circumstances. It left us all knocked for six because we had been on so many patrols together and seen so many successes. Of course I guess it could have been any of us as we had all come close many times, but it never ever reduces the impact. I had known Alex from my first sniper course and remember chatting to him about me joining the snipers when we were in Basra, Iraq. He had even saved a bed space in D Company's lines for me when I finally joined the snipers, and we remained room-mates for just over two years. We used to go down to the local chippy and he would put the chips alongside a fresh steak he had bought from the local Sainsbury's and grilled on his George Foreman grill. We used to discuss the normal stuff like cars, girlfriends and the like, and watch certain TV shows religiously. I guess we just became really good friends. Hopefully you can see why I was so heart-broken by the passing of Alex. We were not simply passing mates.

To sort myself out, I decided to be positive and recall my fondest memories of Alex. This was when we were about to travel to Canada on exercise and were parking our cars in the D Company car park before our departure. There was a slope with a row of trees on one side and Alex parked in front of it. I noticed he had left his hand brake on, so I advised him not to as we were going for six weeks and the handbrake might well have seized up by the time we returned. I told him to leave it in first gear and it would be fine when we returned. He watched me do mine and then did the same himself, feeling quite chuffed. We then walked towards the block and halfway up the stairs he stopped and said, 'Shit, I've got to go and get something.' I just said, 'No problem' and continued up the stairs.

A few minutes later, while I was sorting out my bed space, Alex walked in with a look of horror on his face. He could not even tell me, instead beckoning me to come outside and look. His car was on the slope, a total mangled wreck with the bonnet caved in. It turned out that he had half-sat in the driver's seat to grab the disk he wanted out of the CD player, but needed to start the car up so it would eject. He had of course forgotten that the car was in first gear. It had jolted forward, travelling down the slope and into a tree with such force that it caved in the bonnet. We laughed so much it actually hurt. Probably because of his face but, typical of squaddie mentality, we all laughed and ripped the piss out of him mercilessly, falling about laughing. He just about wet himself laughing too but, as we were flying to Canada in around two hours, there was nothing he could do at all.

My second favourite memory of Alex was when we were in Canada. We had just finished the main exercise and so had a few days of low level administration to sort out, moving things around and packing things up. It was one of those rare occasions when it did not really matter if we went out and got stonking. So all the snipers decided to go out to dinner and chose one of these family franchised restaurants called Montana's. There was Tom, Deano, Spud, Donny, Teddy, me, and of course, Alex. We all managed to use our English charm and sweet-talked the barmaid to allow us to eat our meals at the bar from the bar stools, which was not allowed normally. Alex and I were at one end, with Tom and Deano at the other. Tom and Deano had discovered that if it was anyone's birthday, the restaurant would play these loud sirens, the employees would come out and silly Canadian moose hats would be put on and they would really go for it.

If it was a kid, that would be lovely of course and they would end up simply having a song played and blowing the candles out on a cake. If it was an adult, they would be made to stand on their chair and wear a moose hat in front of everyone and have a pie pushed in their face. Once the boys had realised this, they told the bar staff that it was Alex's birthday and then waited for the fireworks and sirens.

The sirens sounded and Alex watched the moose-hatted staff stroll towards our area singing away, without suspecting for a moment that it was for him. Alex looked over his left shoulder looking for the poor unsuspecting victim and then did the world's greatest double-take as we split ourselves laughing as he looked behind himself and then back at them and then again. When he realised that it was for him, he looked over at Deano and Tom and mouthed one word, 'Wankers!'

The next thing you know, he was being dragged up on his bar stool by the employees and made to wear the moose hat. When they helped him back down, a pie was then splatted in his face. We all laughed for hours.

These were my two best memories of my friend Alex that I chose to play over in my head but neither they nor the other positive thoughts in my head could keep away the pain. The Battalion's padre held a memorial service for Alex where there were many hymns that no one sang apart from the padre. We all stood with our heads down. We were remembering our friend in our own ways; in short, we were all utterly gutted by his death. No mistakes had been made, Alex had simply been in the wrong place at the wrong time. It was a nightmare for all of us although nothing like how his family must have felt.

Alex's repatriation took place a few days later and Teddy was asked to stand up and give a speech, which he of course did. The C-130 Hercules aircraft carrying his body took off from Camp Bastion and then turned, flying northwards towards us. We raised our heads as it thundered overhead, dipping its wings in salute before turning and carrying Alex away on the first stage of his final journey home.

Alex will always be in my memory, sadly missed.

On 1 August, the Battalion celebrated Minden Day, which is the annual major occasion for the Royal Anglian Regiment. This commemorates one of the Royal Anglian Regiment's many battle honours that are emblazoned on the regimental colours. During the Seven Years War, four miles north west of the city of Minden in Westphalia, Duke Ferdinand of Brunswick commanded the Allied Army made up of troops from Britain, Hanover, Hess and Prussia, while Marshal The Marquis Louis de Contades commanded the French Army. The Allied objective was to reopen its communications with Hanover. An ambiguously worded command sent six British and three Hanoverian infantry battalions against the French cavalry while still in line formation, a foolhardy move that should have spelt disaster. Despite this, the discipline and courage of the infantry repelled three French cavalry charges and smashed the French infantry in the centre of Contades's formation. After the battle, which took place on 1 August 1759, the British battalions marched through a field where both yellow and red roses grew. The soldiers each picked one of each colour and put them in their head-dress with the red on the left and the yellow on the right. This stood for courage before dishonour. The six British infantry regiments involved, The Suffolk Regiment, The Royal Hampshire Regiment, The Lancashire Fusiliers, The Royal Welch Fusiliers, The King's Own Yorkshire Light Infantry, and the King's Own Scottish Borderers, thereafter celebrated this victory as a battle honour on Minden Day each year. To this day, our tactical recognition flash (TRF), which is worn on the right sleeve of our shirt or jacket, comprises a red and yellow square that is the Minden flash.

In the UK, Minden Day normally begins at around 8.00 am with the officers of each company dressed up as Vikings storming into our rooms, crashing through the doors and beating us over the heads with foam swords and dragging us from our beds. We are then subjected to downing some 'gunfire' which is tea laced with rum. The trouble is that I hate tea so always ended up downing a glass of neat rum which was fine with me! After that, everyone quickly puts on some PT kit and we would get ourselves downstairs where there was normally some form of comedy act, normally consisting of some Z list celebrity leading us in aerobics on the parade square, during which we would just mess around. This is followed by a parade, with us in our best uniforms, during which citations are read out from the actual original report of exactly what happened on the day of the battle in 1759. During the parade, we attach fake roses in our head-dress and wear them for the rest of the day. In the afternoon an event takes place that I can only describe as being like a village fête, where we all organise a stand. It is full of the normal good fun stuff, with our company commander being put in the stocks and having wet sponges chucked at him, and the Royal British Legion appearing and raffling off a car. Throughout the day there are barbecues and plenty to drink, and by evening time we are all normally pretty well served. Basically, it is normally a day off just before we go on summer leave on 1 August each year and it is great fun.

This time around, of course, we were on operations in Afghanistan on 1 August, so no getting legless. That said, we still made it out on the cement square at Kajaki, which was normally our five-a-side football pitch. We had competitive games where points were awarded, to be totted up at the end of the day, with us in the FSG competing against 5, 6 and 7 Platoons. The FSG stand had been rigged up as a water jousting event for which we had obtained water from the reservoir and fashioned lances from Javelin transit tubes and bits of wood covered with foam padding. Two people stood at either end of a narrow plank, the two of them knocking the crap out of each other until one of them fell off into the water. As we obviously had not brought the traditional fancy dress with us to Afghanistan, we had to improvise. In my case, I fashioned a hula hula skirt from orange mine tape cut into strips and attached to a green felt belt.

The last event was a scrap heap challenge whereby teams used all kinds of junk to build a raft that had to carry its team out from the edge of the reservoir to a tower a good 800 or 900 metres out in the water. It was another good laugh as ours totally fell apart and we all got wet and had to swim back.

That day was a great laugh that I will never forget. We had a big barbecue where the CQMS squared away a few crates of non-alcoholic beer which tasted awful, but it was the only thing to drink that was actually cold, so everyone tucked in. A few guys had gone down to the river and caught loads of beautiful fresh fish, which were lovely on the barbecue and about the only thing that was fresh on the menu. We also had some spam, which we had for breakfast as well. It was a really good crack with lots of banter and laughter, allowing us to wind down just for one day. The most brilliant thing of all was that the FSG won the football by the tightest of margins after an awesome game.

By 10 August, Minden Day seemed like a distant memory because we received some very bad news and the reality of war kicked in once again. Private Tony Rawson, or Nicey as we fondly knew him, was killed in action. As I mentioned earlier, Tony was nicknamed Nicey simply because he was just one of the best blokes you could ever wish to meet. The nickname said it all. The arrival of a new recruit would capture the kind of guy he was, as he would always be the one that would go and shake hands with them and show them around with that Essex charm he had. He did not have to do this, and the rest of us sometimes could be cautious until we knew that the new arrivals were okay, so to the poor buggers that came without knowing a soul he must have been a godsend. I knew Nicey from my time with C Company when I first joined.

What had happened was that C Company was in the process of clearing the Jucelay and Putay areas while further work continued on FOB Inkerman work could begin on constructing a forward operating base to stop the Taliban from infiltrating back into the area. The Taliban were really pushing hard to get back into Sangin and so C Company was seeing a lot of action down there, with contacts in the Green Zone occurring almost on a daily basis. Sadly our good friend Nicey was killed during one of these. We were all gutted by his death.

On the following day Captain David Hicks, the acting commander of C Company, was killed during a Taliban attack on FOB Inkerman. The Taliban had managed to lay their hands on a quantity of Russian SPG-9 tripod-mounted 73mm recoilless anti-tank guns, which they mounted on the backs of pick-up trucks. It was a round from one of these that exploded close to Captain Hicks while he was in a sangar, attempting to identify five enemy firing positions. Despite being very seriously wounded, he picked himself up and began organising a counter-attack, refusing medical attention as he did so. Unfortunately, he died of wounds shortly after the arrival of the chopper that brought in a medical emergency response team. Subsequently he was quite rightly awarded a posthumous Military Cross. He was a very courageous man, a real leader and a kind of typical officer with a chiselled jaw and posh accent but absolutely one of the guys as well. He possessed a really rare quality as he was one of the very few officers who managed to maintain the necessary distance, yet still be able to speak with you informally. He was one of those who, when he asked you how you were, he really meant it. It was a real tragedy that he lost his life.

The mood was understandably sombre as we resumed patrolling. This time we were deployed on a patrol to the south where once again we positioned ourselves up on the ridgeline with some GPMGs, with Corporal Si Thorn in charge of the gun line. There were some Americans present. I am not sure if they were part of Task Force Fury, but they were in the area and not involved with our operation, merely monitoring the situation. On this occasion, they were taking a spectator's seat to pass information back on things like tactics of the Taliban, anything new, how we Brits were tackling them and anything else that was helpful to their own people. They were a really good laugh and great guys.

The normal situation ensued, with the Taliban shooting at us from the Green Zone and then moving back to their own headquarters location, followed by us putting down fire and then traversing it to allow our guys on the ground to push forward. We did not want a blue-on-blue situation with us hitting our own men, and it was difficult to spot where the Taliban were down in amongst the trees. This said, we had been out there so long that our eyes had got used to what we were observing. Everything really stood out when we watched the area. I was looking through my scope towards the Taliban headquarters and zapped it with my rangefinders and they came up showing a range of 1,000 metres-plus as these things measured out to a distance of kilometre away. I began moving them down and zapped a few buildings at around 900 metres.

I was about to move on when I spotted a muzzle flash in one of the windows in a building. I zapped it again and the range was approximately 920 metres, so I prepared my rifle, which was an L96 on this patrol. I remembered from when we were in FOB Robinson that I was able to hit a track around a kilometre away, so reckoned I would be able to shoot within five metres of the target and put a round in there. If nothing else, it would make him get his head down for a bit and take some heat off our guys by stopping him from shooting. I tried to call over to Teddy to let him know I had someone a kilometre away, but the GPMGs were really thundering away and everyone was occupied, so I thought I would just crack on.

I began to line up my scope. I was watching the window but hadn't seen any more flashes from it, so thought maybe the target had moved. I waited and waited until he suddenly appeared in the doorway, dropped to one knee and fired a burst of rounds. I had the range dialled into the scope along with the corrected windage, so took my shot which impacted slightly sort to the right as I saw the dust kick up from the ground. With this, he darted back inside the building. I reloaded and continued to watch. Suddenly, I saw him appear from the back of the building and begin to run into open ground. There was a dip in the ground surrounded by rocks and he stopped there to fire some rounds. I zapped the rocks and the range was further away at 1,000-plus. I put maximum clicks on my scope, added the windage, aimed high just a bit extra then fired. I hit him square from around a kilometre away! I could not believe it as I watched him fall back. It must have been one of the luckiest shots ever as it was such a distance away. I was cheering like England had won the World Cup and people were asking what I was on about, with me telling them that I had a hit a guy down there. Luckily, you could still see his leg and feet as he had fallen back into the dip in the ground. Anyway it was a good result and I was very happy with myself.

Teddy, Troy and I chatted to the Americans back at base that night about the best army in the world and what it would comprise. In the end, we all agreed that it would consist of German officers, British soldiers and American money and equipment. We all laughed as we reasoned that, if you stripped away the political side and horrible reasons for the Second World War and just focused on tactics and quality of soldiering on a professional level, the German officers were very good indeed. We had read various books about the North Africa campaign and the blitzkrieg and I was happy to admit that the German officers and also the German snipers were the best. We all agreed on the British soldier because basically you do not get much better than his true grit. In my opinion, we normally have the odds stacked against us because, although we currently do have some fantastic kit in the

British Army, in 2007 the issue kit and equipment either fell apart or was not comfortable so we always had to modify and tinker and overcome the problems with it. At that time a lot of guys bought a lot of their own kit too, myself included. The American military, on the other hand, appears to be well funded and really does have awesome kit and weapons.

The next patrol we conducted was out to a place called Chinah. We were accompanied by some press from London who also did a small article on Teddy. As he was such a prolific sniper with over twenty kills notched up, they were keen to talk to him. These guys were behaving near enough suicidally as they kept jumping up to see what was happening. The worst one of the lot was the cameraman who seemed to forget these were live bullets that were being fired at them. They had some guys assigned to look after them and it was amusing listening to them from behind, shouting to the press guys, 'Get your f...ing head down, you twat!' We all had the utmost respect and regard for any civilian who came out voluntarily, just to bring the reality back to the British people. We all had a lot of time for Ross Kemp as he put himself on the front line to make his documentaries which showed people at home what we were doing. Anyway, it was an interesting exercise trying to 'babysit' the press whilst being in a fire fight with the Taliban; those press guys were great lads and we all appreciated what they were doing. They asked us the normal kind of questions, such as, 'Are you homesick?' and, 'How do you feel knowing that each time you go out, you might not come back?' and things like that. They also asked us if we knew why we were there and if we thought it was a good idea, which we answered honestly.

After that, we patrolled right to the far north and could see people moving out towards a compound. We had not yet identified it as a potential Taliban headquarters, but it was looking more and more likely as there were women and children hanging around and a few guys of fighting age between eighteen and thirty who stood in doorways looking out. They were a hell of a long way out but, using the trusty Leopold scope on 40x, we could observe a group of people outside the compound looking at the area we occupied. The strange thing was that the whole area was just dead and we were wondering whether the Taliban were there and why they were not shooting at us.

We sat and waited for a while, wondering if they were perhaps sneaking up on us to launch a surprise attack, but nothing happened until eventually a few people turned up. Corporal Kennedy heard some rustling and sat up on the wall immediately, his safety catch off and rifle at the ready, only to see an old Afghan herding some goats. He was very lucky he did not have anything on him that resembled a gun, or anything in his hands slightly out of sight, because Corporal Kennedy was really close to dropping him as he thought it was someone creeping up on us.

We observed people moving between buildings, but could not see any weapons, which surprised and made us slightly on edge as it was all so unusual. There was one guy that was moving towards us between the buildings. I had chiselled out a loophole in the edge of a building where there was a parapet like the one in Jucelay, and was watching the guy through it. I did not know at the time but Teddy had also spotted him, so we were both tracking him. I zapped him with the rangefinders and he was around 450 or 500 metres away when he stopped and raised his hand to shield his eyes from the sun. He turned slightly to the right and I had to really squint and look hard, but was pretty sure I could see the barrel of a weapon poking out from his robes and the outline of a weapon. I asked Sergeant Chris Caneper, who was with me, to have a look and confirm and as he agreed that he could see something.

Teddy had also seen it and fired a few seconds before I did. The shot narrowly missed as the guy darted back towards a building. He was a fast moving target 500 metres away, so really hard to hit but Teddy reloaded and fired, missing again as I fired and watched my bullet impact literally right next to his toes. He managed to reach a doorway leaving Teddy and me absolutely gutted. The guy was such a lucky bastard and I guessed he would thank Allah for being a bloody fast runner.

We did not see or hear anything else, so could not justify an air strike based on just this one guy, but it was all a bit strange. We had now been up since 3.00 am and it was now around 10.00 am, so we were all starving and somewhat tired. As I was thinking this, Major Borgnis walked over, sat down next to me and said, 'I don't know. What do you think, Lance Corporal Cartwright?'

I was a bit taken aback that the new OC knew my name so well. Anyway I told him that I thought it was definitely slightly strange. He looked at me and said, 'Can we go home then?' I thought, 'What!' I looked back as all his tactical staff and minions glared down at me. He asked, 'Are you hungry?' I paused before replying, 'Er... yes.' He then said, 'Do you want some breakfast, Lance Corporal Cartwright?' I must have looked confused and asked if this was a trick question, to which he replied, 'No, no, just answer honestly.' So I said, "To be honest with you, yes. I'm absolutely starving, sir.'

With that, he called up on the radio and said, 'All call signs, we are ready to move back now, let's call it a day.' He then went to his PRR and added, 'Just for the record, it was Lance Corporal Cartwright's decision and he gave us permission to move out, so thank him because he's hungry.' He stood up and gave me a little wink and laughed, as did all his minions. I thought, 'This guy is actually bloody good,' and laughed as well. It made a nice refreshing change as we began the long hard slog back to FOB Zeebrugge and some lovely ravioli and spam.

CHAPTER 17

Blue on Blue

A few days later, Major Borgnis came over to Teddy and me, and asked us if we thought we could locate and kill the enemy sniper who had been operating in the area. We told him that we knew he was using a .50 calibre sniper rifle but that was all we had on him, and decided to suss out a possible plan. In ideal circumstances we would pretty much use the whole of the Sniper Platoon, which numbered around seventeen snipers, and set up an OP screen to sit and wait for him. It is really like a game of chess, and it takes a lot of snipers and a lot of time to catch just the one guy. We told Major Borgnis that for the two of us to find this one sniper in this massive area around Kajaki was almost impossible, unless we were incredibly lucky. It would take a long time and we would have to draw him out into an area where we actually wanted him, rather than trying to just catch him out.

The only way we could do this was to have the use of a couple of platoons to go forward and engage the enemy. Simply advance to contact and, when the enemy starts to fire back, just hold their ground there. Whilst this would be happening, Teddy and I would take two different angles and look into the main contact area. We already knew that he was operating from the flanks, so if he were going to engage us from a built-up area it was going to make our job more difficult as there were simply more places to hide there. Taking all into consideration, we felt that this would be the best option. Major Borgnis said, 'Well okay, if we can get this sniper it's worth a shot.'

It was not just a case of removing this sniper for our tour, but also for future operations and tours that came after us. The OC was happy for our help and went away to form his plan. Teddy and I sat around the table thinking about dealing with the sniper. We were like kids imagining if we got him, because if we found him, killed him and recovered his rifle, then in our sniper world this would be like winning the World Cup. We agreed that we would dedicate our feat to the Corporals' Mess and have a plaque mounted on the mess bar saying where the sniper was killed and his rifle was retrieved by sniper from OP HERRICK 6. We went on like that for some time and it was nice to lose ourselves in fantasy for a while. The reality, of course, would be very different as the sniper was not about to hand over his life and rifle that easily and that we would have to go and take him on, kill him and secure his weapon.

The next day, Major Borgnis had taken our advice and gone with it, which made us feel really good and we relished the opportunity. He told us that he was not going to spend a huge amount of time and effort to dealing with the sniper, but would give it a go with this one attempt.

So late one afternoon, we set off. It was not too hot as the temperature was cooling. 6 and 7 Platoons moved up to Masdurak and took up their positions. Teddy was with the WMIKs and I was with 6 Platoon as it advanced. Teddy, equipped with his .338 rifle, was quite close to the FSG while I, with my L96, accompanied the main body of the patrol. We pushed through and looked over Masdurak and the big wadi, going firm in the positions we took up. I asked one of the guys to keep looking into the windows of buildings and scanning the entire area as best he could from the mound of rubble on which he was lying. As he was doing so, there was a shot and a bullet cracked past his head. He scrambled down with a wide-eyed stare as I sat there savouring the sound of the unmistakable crack and thump of a sniper rifle. Our man was here!

We swiftly deployed in amongst the rubble that is Masdurak and found an area with a few mouseholes, the scene looking like the bombed streets of London during the Second World War. After that one shot it sounded like it too as all hell broke loose, with RPGs being launched from the enemy's side with our guys returning fire across the wadi exactly as planned. The sniper had already identified himself as being here and it was now down to Teddy and me to find him in amongst the mayhem. It dawned on me that we would never be able to lay our hands on his rifle in this situation, but we could at least try and achieve a confirmed enemy sniper kill.

I was alternating through three positions because if you remain in one for too long you are just asking for it. I could only identify muzzle flashes in windows, so it was really difficult to identify the actual sniper. What's more, I could not out look properly as there were bullets ricocheting off of the rubble and whizzing past my head, while dust and rubble were being thrown up all over the place, making if difficult to sit there calmly engaging targets. There were RPGs coming in so we frequently had to take cover and wait until they exploded, being showered with rocks and dust before we could crack on again. After about twenty or thirty minutes of this, we had not located our target and it was impossible for us to know if he was even still out there. The volume of noise from the continuing barrage of gunfire and explosions was such that it was difficult to pinpoint specific noises, while the visibility grew worse from the smoke and dust.

The message eventually came down the line that the JTAC was going to have a few bombs dropped in order that we could withdraw, so we hoped we might knock out the sniper by dropping a bloody great bomb on him. The guy next to me had been hammering away with his Minimi, so his hearing at this point was absolutely shot. So there I was, shouting at him with large mouth movements and doing sign language to warn him. I was mouthing the words, 'AMEEEEERICAAAAN, F-15 DROPPING BOMMMMMMB FIIIIIVE MINUTES!!!' No matter how hard I shouted he was still saying, 'Hey! What?' so in the end I extracted my notebook and pen and wrote it down for him, 'Bomb, five minutes', at which he stuck his thumb up and carried on firing. Good lad. Within what seemed about ten seconds, I received the call that the bomb was going in and we had about two minutes, so I held up two fingers and he nodded again.

I heard a very loud noise and, looking round, could just about make out the jet coming in. I could hear the roar of his engines getting louder and louder as he came from behind us. He dropped his bomb as we all took cover and the ground literally shook as the bomb went off. Everyone did the normal 'Woo hooo!' as it exploded but this bomb was very, very close to us and even though we had a lot of experience of close air support, this one just seemed too near. I looked up to see a big cloud of smoke on our side of the wadi and told the guy with the Minimi to wait there as the platoon sergeant was just through an archway. Seconds later, he confirmed my worst fears that it was a 'blue-on-blue' – casualties caused by friendly fire.

Firing ceased on both sides as I think the Taliban, as well as ourselves, could not believe what had happened. We had seen the enemy score an own goal and blow themselves up through a dodgy mortar on a number of occasions, but for us to have a bomb dropped on us by a supporting aircraft was a tragedy for us and a godsend for them.

I was with 6 Platoon and Sergeant Browning was telling us that 7 Platoon was down there, separated from us by only a few buildings. The bomb had landed no more than a 100 metres away from us. Then we began to hear the radio transmissions come through. 'We have one T4, a couple of T1s and a couple of T2s.' At this point, Major Borgnis wanted to begin the extraction plan as the Taliban had recovered and were beginning to cross the wadi towards us as they realised that we would clearly be in a certain degree of shock and wanted to take advantage of the situation. Some of our guys were putting down fire while others were busy guiding the members of 7 Platoon bringing their wounded out of the maze of alleyways to the Pinzgauers. In the meantime, a Chinook was already on its way to pick them up and take them to Camp Bastion for medical treatment. We also had to get the dead out, as it had already been confirmed that we had one dead in our ranks. I scribbled a note to my deaf friend next to me saying, 'Blue-on-blue, we are pulling out.' He looked confused, wanting to know what had happened.

The platoon sergeant was busy organising men to stand at certain alleyways and cover us while also giving directions to the teams bringing out the dead and wounded. They had to improvise by using ponchos for stretchers as we had a growing list of casualties with another T1 joining the group. On one such makeshift stretcher was my friend and comrade, Josh Lee. His clothes were burned and ripped, his face covered in dust. As I watched the guys carrying him out, I could see he was not moving much but there was nothing I could do apart from give encouragement to the guys carrying him to keep going and push on quickly. The next to come out was someone I had fought alongside so many times, Corporal Stuart 'Parky' Parker. His clothes were in a similar state but at least he was moving, which was a good sign. He had his eyes clamped shut and was moving his head from side to side, but the worrying thing was that his chest was dark blue and red. Once again, there was nothing any of us could do apart from give words of encouragement to the guys carrying him.

I turned and came across a good mate of mine, Luke Geater, and he just looked at me and told me that Troy was dead. I stood for a few seconds and then turned and kicked the wall next to me, which was stupid as I nearly broke my foot but I just didn't care. Luke put his arm around me and we just stood there for a few more seconds as I tried to deal with it all mentally. I broke away and asked who else was dead and I heard the words from him and then another guy who confirmed that Privates Thrumble and McClure were both dead. I was just totally gutted. Major Borgnis came through with the JTAC and of course the boys' eyes became daggers as the man who had ordered the air strike walked through. In fairness, it was the right thing to call in air support and the JTAC was not in the pilot's seat. As he walked through, he said with genuine sincerity that he was sorry, so sorry as he walked through us. I felt for him as he went through apologising. It was not his fault and I for one knew that. All of them felt as bad as us, as they obviously would never have deliberately perpetrated anything like that on their own guys. It was just one of those things. When someone in civilian life makes a mistake it is usually just a pain in the arse but everyone gets over it. When we make a mistake, it costs lives and affects everyone. I shook my head in disbelief, thinking of the men now dead as the JTAC walked past and we began to move back.

The sun was setting now and it was beginning to get really dark.

We were out of Masdurak and our mortar line was beginning to bring down fire on the Taliban as we withdrew under cover of smoke from the mortars and arrived at a different wadi. The dead and wounded had been driven away. Everyone was so down about what had happened. We did what we would call a 'hard extraction' and ran all the way back to FOB Zeebrugge which, although totally exhausting, helped take our minds off what had happened. Just before we arrived at the base, we organised all round defence at the village of Tangey to receive the Chinook helicopter which arrived to pick up the wounded and dead to take them back to Camp Bastion.

When I got back in, I saw Teddy and watched as he just sat with his head in his hands. I put my hand on his shoulder and said that it was f...ing shit and he said, 'Yeah, really f...ing shit.' He lit a cigarette and I did too. Behind us was the kit of the guys who had died, their day sacks ripped and torn, and John Thrumble's GPMG bent and mangled. As we looked at this, the call came around asking if anyone had seen Private Foster. None of us had seen him and the problem was that Stu Parker had been his section commander and Josh Lee the second-in-command. It swiftly became clear that no head count had been completed for this section. We very soon realised that Fozzy was missing in action, so a search party was organised immediately, with some of A Company being flown in from Sangin to help us.

It was now totally dark with lots of Taliban in the area by now. Nevertheless, the guys still went back to the scene of the blue-on-blue and, after digging in the rubble, found Fozzy. He was dead. He had been firing from the compound through a loophole and had taken almost the full force of the blast. If it was any consolation to us, he would have died instantly and not have suffered, but it was still soul destroying for yet another of us to fall. There were three great guys killed in action through this blue-on-blue, friendly fire or whatever you want to call it. The thing that was so upsetting was that the four guys we lost in B Company all died through tragic accidents rather than being shot by the enemy. Sometimes that is what makes war that little bit harder to take. We were warned during training that not all of us would come home, and were told, 'Just do your best to make sure it is not you or the people to your right and left.' It is a difficult thing to deal with when any comrades die, but especially your good friends. The mentality that was drilled into us, came naturally anyway, was work hard for each other and fight for each other. The standard things we heard were Queen, Country and Patriotism but these meant nothing to us. We did not even care why we were there as all that mattered was being there for each other while we were fighting. We were all there together and for each other and doing our job.

Teddy was a trained medic and had helped by working on Stu Parker and Josh Lee, ensuring they were kept alive during the Golden Hour before the helicopter arrived. It is testament to these two guys that, during the care being given to them, they continually kept asking about their soldiers and how they were. Teddy had to lie to them as they asked about Troy and Thrumble. He did not want to cause them any more shock or stress as they were clearly very badly wounded, keeping them as calm as possible while they were given first aid. He helped load them on to the Chinook and, as he did so, saw a hand wearing a distinctive glove protruding from under a covering sheet. It was Troy. Teddy had lent him those gloves when Troy said he liked them. Teddy had a spare pair so Troy could have kept them, and now he would.

This all happened on 23 August 2007 and I will never forget it.

There was an Op MINIMIZE put in place, barring anyone from speaking to the outside world, but I managed to speak to Annie a few days later on her birthday. I had ordered an Arsenal shirt with 'Daddy's Girl' and a number one on the back, and she had received this in time for her birthday, which was great stuff. When I talked to her, she told me that she and my Mum had all obviously heard about the blue-on-blue, through the national news, so they asked me if I knew any of them. I remember saying that I knew all of them and they were my friends. They were brilliant soldiers and great men. It pisses me off when I hear news reports about horrible men doing terrible things who are sent to go to prison for only a few years, whereas these guys were nice men who had put their lives on the line and would not be coming back.

A day or so later the CO and RSM came out and saw us. Ross Kemp also arrived. Having spent time with these guys, he had insisted on coming back which was good of him. They were not simply names on a newsreel to him or any of us. It was really nice for the guys from the head shed to come down and spend time with us after this, and it was much appreciated by the men.

We also had some journalists from New York come out on patrol with us and they were a lot less trouble than our lovely Brits, being slightly less suicidal than our lot and actually listening to what we told them. Eventually the call came through that 7 Platoon were going to move to Sangin with some of the FSG guys so they could man the FSG tower in Sangin DC, whilst A Company was going to deploy on Operation PALK GHAR, which was to last from 30 August to 2 September.

Snowy asked for some volunteers to go and help man the tower at Sangin and I stuck my hand up. Privates Tanner 'TT' Tremain and 'Ghost Face' Read also volunteered. Two days before we were due to fly out, Ghost Face and TT were up the top of the hill in OP Sparrow Hawk and I, along with Private Bernie Turner and a few other guys, was tasked with taking a few Javelin missiles and some GPMG ammunition up there. The ground either side of the track was mined, so you could not under any circumstances stray off the track. The trouble was that it was as narrow as a cricket bat in some places, so all of us were treading carefully. We all had to wear our body armour, but could take off our helmets. Bernie Turner and I were ahead of the others marching up the hill. He slipped and, as he put his hand out to break the fall, his helmet slipped from it and bounced down the hill. We were pissing ourselves with laughter as we put our fingers in our ears and watched the helmet bouncing down the hill while waiting for an explosion if it hit a mine. The trouble was, he had to go home in four days on his R & R and needed a helmet to travel. He was gutted, as he was convinced he would not be permitted to travel home without it, but I said, 'Don't worry, I'm sure one of the guys will be able to get you a helmet from somewhere.' That happened of course and Bernie went on his R & R while his helmet remained in the middle of the minefield.

Before we left for Sangin DC, Teddy gave me a letter to pass on to his loved ones, just in case he did not make it, while I gave him a similar letter for Annie. We promised to pass these on should the worst happen, smoked a cigarette together, shook and hands and then I boarded the Chinook for Sangin.

When we arrived, TT, Ghost Face and I were shown in to the room we would be occupying in the DC building. I then decided to go and find the FSG snipers and walked around looking for them. Sure enough, there in the corner was our platoon commander, Colour Sergeant 'Fruity' Faupel, OB, Jimmy and Donny. Jock had been repatriated back to the UK because of injury. Although it was nothing more serious than an injured ankle, he clearly could not even walk properly, let alone patrol, so he had been sent back. It was so good seeing these guys, listening to their stories and catching up with what they had been up to. They were due to move out on Operation PALK GHAR and were to clear the area around Jucelay as FOB Inkerman had now been properly built since we had cleared that area during Operation LASTAY KULANG. The Taliban really wanted to maintain a stranglehold on the top of Sangin. Even though we had cleared the area and build forward operating bases there, we had trouble maintaining it and had to sweep the ground again and leave more men there. Both C Company and A Company were involved in the operation, so they needed the towers at Sangin manned in their absence.

We kept back various guys who had suffered non-serious injuries to stay and help man Sangin. There was really good surveillance from the CCTV cameras covering the area and we logged any activity that we could detect. It was pretty uneventful but there were a few times when we supported various incidents. It was actually a bit of a relief to see the tracer rounds in the distance and realise that for a change it was not us on the receiving end. It was more like being a spectator, listening to the traffic on the radio net and monitoring what was happening in different areas rather than being in the thick of the action, on top of roofs, or shooting and moving while being shot at.

Ross Kemp came out again to conduct some interviews while I was with the other guys living in the tower and manning the sangars. 7 Platoon meanwhile was living in the old mortar area that was in the other part of Sangin on the opposite side of the canal where we all used to swim and wash. We all went over there with Ross and organised a barbecue. OD set it up and we sat around it with Ross and his camera crew. We baked some bread after managing to get some bread mixture from the chefs, and caught some fish from the canal to grill. We talked through what happened and how we felt about the blue-on-blue. You could tell that Ross really did actually care about us guys and in a way felt that he too had lost some friends.

CHAPTER 18

Sniper Ops

Fruity came back from PALK GHAR and told me something that made my day. I was not going back to Kajaki, but was to accompany him to Camp Bastion. I said, 'Really?' He replied, 'Yes, we are going to be doing sniper ops.' I was so chuffed and asked what this involved. Fruity said he was not sure but the entire Sniper Platoon was going to operate as one unit. The CO had not used the platoon as an entity up until now but we were now entering the last four weeks of this tour, so he went for it. Teddy was to get a flight back from Kajaki to Camp Bastion, so it was all spot on – in fact absolutely brilliant. I gave the rest of my MRE ration packs to Ghost Face and TT and readied myself for a life of luxury at Camp Bastion: hot showers, fresh food, laundry service and air conditioning. It was like moving to a five star hotel.

The other guys were so jealous. I told Sergeant Woodrow about the move and he said, 'No worries, have fun.' After the formalities were over, he called me a lucky, cheeky bastard. I remember thinking, 'Yep, happy with that.' Nothing was going to bring me down as I was going to meet the entire sniper platoon in the luxury of Camp Bastion. It was a great day.

I waved Ghost Face, TT and the rest of the guys off as they flew away towards Kajaki and then remained waiting at the flight line until another Chinook arrived. Within five minutes I was in the air over Sangin and on my way to Bastion.

On arrival, I was met by Sergeant Major Terry Taylor who was in command of the Reconnaissance Platoon which was back at Bastion at the time because its vehicles had broken down. As there were only a few weeks left of the tour, there was no major hurry to repair and redeploy them. The major operations for this tour had all finished and, as we were now into September, with the next unit due to arrive at the end of the month to begin its tour, things were now finally beginning to wind down for us.

Fruity, Donny, OB, Jimmy and I all jumped into Sergeant Major Taylor's Pinzgauer and before long I was off loading all my stuff. I soon saw that everyone in the platoon was there – Teddy, Robbo, Tom, Kingy, Mo, DG, Sarge, Cas and the rest. It was so good to see everyone in one place and soon we were all shaking hands and talking about our experiences. The atmosphere was fantastic and it was like an old school boys' reunion, which was great after all that we had been through. Sergeant Major Taylor then told us what was going to happen. The Sniper Platoon was going to be doing OP work, which was our bread and butter role, with the Recce Platoon deploying with us as a quick reaction force (QRF).

While the head shed planned what we were going to be doing, we took advantage of life in Camp Bastion. While most civilians are used to having time off at weekends, for us it was paradise to have a few days with nothing to do because weekends and bank holidays do not exist on operational tours. Our weapons were cleaned, to the point that they may as well have been new, before being stowed away. We showered and put our clothes in the launderette, which for us was just absolutely brilliant, and played cards and drank cans of ice cold coke. Having a shower in the morning and another in the evening was also just sheer luxury, as was being able to have a chocolate bar that was solid and not a fluid mess. Silly things like that meant so much to us. We also had a Pizza Hut open up, and even had a Play Station 2 and a television so everything just felt like a whole world away from the last six months. Furthermore, I found that I was actually able to sleep because the air conditioning was really working, so we had to zip up our sleeping bags and could sleep, really sleep, for the first time in what seemed an age.

This wonderful interlude was only to last for three days and soon we were preparing for the last operations of the tour, which would throw up some real surprises.

The first operation that we were to carry out involved an enemy sniper operating in the Nowzad area where the Taliban had, for all intents and purposes, freedom of movement around the area doing what they wanted while our guys were largely confined to the DC. Although we had pushed the buffer zone out from where the Marines had left it, the Taliban could still re-infiltrate the area. It had been decided to put out an OP screen around Nowzad. We established this on the outside of the DC while a third OP was set up in one of the sangars on the corner of the district centre. A QRF was formed of eight guys from the Recce Platoon, under the command of Sergeant Major Terry Taylor, its role being to react swiftly to any threat outside the wire. We had received orders that this operation was going to last around four days with the aim of disrupting any Taliban activity.

We had a lot to squeeze in within a short amount of time so, with all our orders sorted and all the kit we needed squared away, we flew out to Nowzad by Chinook and established ourselves in the DC. A platoon from C Company was in Nowzad and it was good to see a couple of faces that I had not seen for a while. The Recce Platoon had managed to acquire a large inflatable thing like a large paddling pool and filled it with water, so at any one time there would usually be a few guys in there trying to cool themselves off in the intense heat.

We reported to the briefing room and were given our final orders. Fruity was to be in charge of his section, with Donny as the 2IC, OB and JL. We were left with twelve snipers as we had lost Alex and a few others had been injured, while Robbo had been sent home early to do some courses. In our section there was Mo, Teddy, Kingy and me. We split up into three groups of four. In the second OP there was our Platoon Sergeant, Tom, Cas and DG.

We carried out a patrol round the outside of the DC, just to familiarise ourselves with the surroundings, and looked into various buildings. That night the Recce Platoon went out in a couple of WMIKs while we deployed into our respective OPs. We established ourselves in our sangar where we remained for four days. Being inside the wire, we had the luxury of being able to have a cigarette if we went down the ladder right to the bottom of the sangar. The guys on the outside had to do the stint on 'hard routine' with no cigarettes. At night, we avoided the use of torches or lights completely for obvious reasons.

One night, during one of my stags, I was sitting in the chair with a bottle of juice by my side while looking through the night vision equipment. I put the bottle to my lips only to recoil from the most disgusting taste, almost like lead or graphite. I spat it out trying my absolute hardest not to throw up as a horrible oily liquid ran down my chin. Teddy heard the quiet commotion and asked what was wrong, only for me to explain that I had just taken a mouthful of Britain's finest gun oil. In the darkness, my juice bottle felt identical in shape and weight. The guys just killed themselves laughing and proceed to take the piss nicely. It was so very good to be back in amongst the platoon again and it felt like old times before we deployed when we were together on exercise. Obviously where we were and what we were doing was a whole different world to exercises, but it felt great to be with my fellow snipers and share a few laughs with them, even if this one was at my expense.

After four days, we withdrew the OP screen. It had all been somewhat uneventful but we did identify two sniper locations that looked directly into the sangars. The Taliban had been somewhat unprofessional by leaving some empty casings on the ground in the positions. We could see that this particular casing was likely to be from a Dragunov sniper rifle and we marked the positions on our maps, so that the next time any of our guys came under fire they would know where to hit first. We moved back to Camp Bastion to prepare for an operation in our next location, which would be Sangin. We had another few days sitting around, chatting and playing poker while the head shed planned the operation. Around this time, Scotty flew back into Afghanistan after being out of action for a long time as a result of accidentally shooting himself in one of his hands. Fruity took him to one side to have a word with him, as he was massively annoyed that there had been a negligent discharge. As a punishment, Scotty spent the last few weeks of the tour working out of Bastion sorting mail and things like this, which must have pissed him off no end.

After being in Afghanistan for so long now, we noticed that our bodies had become acclimatised to the heat because we were not sweating all the time any more but only when we were running around or were wearing our helmets. In any case, we were now in the middle of September when, although it would still be unbearable for those who had not acclimatised, it had cooled slightly and was not that bad for us.

We had to be aware of the enemy at all times although, as the summer came to an end, the pace seemed to change for us and we knew that a lot of the Taliban were now retreating back to the relative safety of the mountains for the winter and to tend the poppy harvest. This did not mean that there was a sudden peace and no enemy were active, far from it, but I guess we just felt it was a little quieter.

In due course we received our orders and deployed to Sangin where we were accommodated in the old mortar compound, the same place as before when Ross Kemp had been with us. I looked at the rooms and it took me back to when it was just so hot that we could not sleep inside. There were a few guys who still preferred to doss down under the camouflage nets, but I preferred to sleep in the building. Dan, Mo and I all slept in the same room and in the evenings would sit around an open fire and chat away. One night we found some old ammunition tins with the extra charges you can clip on to mortar bombs, so I found a piece of plywood and placed some grains of cordite on it, spelling out 'Snipers', and then lit it. This worked really well, the burning grains leaving the word in scorched lettering, so we hung the piece of wood up so everyone around knew who we were.

We received orders to move down to Patrol Base Waterloo for about a week to carry out night standing OPs. This is where we would wait until the sun went down and it was pitch black before going out and setting up two main OPs and a third in reserve to watch the rear. Then a few hours before sunrise, we would withdraw, patrol back to base and sleep during the day. We would become nocturnal creatures for a week. We loaded up the Vector vehicles, which were a newer version of the Pinzgauer, and together with the Recce Platoon in some newly acquired WMIKs drove towards Patrol Base Waterloo. When we arrived, we met the guys relieving the OMLT. They had recently arrived in Afghanistan and seeing their pasty white faces made us realise that it really would be home time for us soon. They asked loads of questions about the tour and what to expect. They had a number of Afghan National Army under them, the OMLT's role being to teach the Afghans how to fight and be professional soldiers. The ultimate aim was for the ANA eventually to take over and fend for themselves, looking after the safety and security of their country.

When we went out for the first night, there was a graveyard on top of the hill that overlooked the 611 road. There was to be a convoy coming through soon, so we were going to spend every night that week watching out for any suspicious activity and ensuring that the Taliban were not coming out under the cover of darkness, planting IEDs and mines or doing anything else which might jeopardise the convoy's safety. On the first night we were in the rear OP on the edge of the graveyard, allowing ourselves only gentle whispering about what we would do when we got home as we kept our eyes to the rear. The hours ticked past before we eventually packed up and withdrew back to base. This continued, with us rotating through the two forward OPs watching the road on subsequent nights.

Not a lot happened, until one night we had withdrawn and were only around 100 metres away from the entrance to Patrol Base Waterloo when out of nowhere there was a sudden crack right over our heads, the familiar sound of incoming rounds. We sprang into action and ran over the bridge and took up firing positions. We waited and waited but nothing happened, which we thought was a bit strange. It transpired that one of the ANA guys inside the base had fired a warning shot over the top of our heads as he was not sure whether we were Taliban. As we ran over the bridge he had realised that we were British troops and apologised. We just thought, 'What a prat!'

The other slight problem associated with the Afghans was their personal hygiene which was, let's just say, not on par with ours. We had a nasty round of diarrhoea and vomiting which spread through the base. I came down with it really badly and even had to sit one of the nights out. I lay in my sleeping bag thinking that, if anything happened to my guys while I was not there, I would have let the team down. Fortunately, nothing occurred and they came back safely. We spoke to some of the ANA guys and gave them some dollars to go and get some locally made fresh bread. They also came back with some local Afghan crisps, which were basically a really cheap version of Wotsits, the cheesy puff crisps back home. You would put one in your mouth and it would evaporate instantly, so you only had a split second of taste and then air. The iPods did the rounds as people got bored of the same playlist over and over again, so we swapped so as to listen to something different. Listening to the music made me realise that I could sense I had changed as a person. I used to listen to the fast paced stuff, but now preferred the more calm type of music.

I was also thinking about Annie and settling down and knew that I did not want to lose her. I began going through things in my mind, having already decided that I was going to propose to her when I arrived home; maybe not straight away, but during something like a nice weekend break to Paris or somewhere equally suitable to pop the question. There was a general feeling of things coming to an end and I was thinking mainly about just making it through the next few weeks and staying alive. Fortunately, nothing happened during the remaining seven days of night standing OPs as there was no one to intercept. The convoy came through safely and there were no nasty surprises lying in wait for it. This was mainly due to Patrol Base Waterloo being such a domineering presence in the area and also that the ANA patrolled the area so effectively and contributed to keeping the Taliban away.

When we left the patrol base and returned to Sangin, the difference in the atmosphere was really noticeable. There were many more people, it was busier and had bustling streets, markets and cars like a proper thriving town. When we had first arrived, the place was almost like a ghost town and only people who were unable, or could not be bothered, to walk out of Sangin remained there. The Taliban were rife before we kicked them out and allowed the town to breathe again. There were even women walking around in groups at the market stalls in their burqas, which we had never seen before as they were always hidden away. It really seemed as though the people had been given their freedom back, which was good. We felt like that we were not wasting our time and were changing the lives of these people for the better.

On our return, we chilled out for a while and had another big barbecue with loads of fresh food and swam in the canal again. We made some fresh bread and had ourselves a bit of a feast before we loaded ourselves back into the vehicles and making our way to FOB Inkerman, better known as FOB In-coming due to the amount of attention it received from the Taliban. Diarrhoea and vomiting was rumoured to be rife there and I was keen to avoid another bout as I was only just getting over the former. I dosed myself up to the maximum on Imodium while also eating large quantities of the biscuits in our ration packs to try to block myself up again. In the meantime, a freshly arrived group of Marines had arrived and were asking loads of questions about the tour.

Everywhere we went, there were new people and new faces arriving. I was counting down the days as I was scheduled to arrive back in the UK on 6 October, which would mean that I would leave Afghanistan on around 1 and 2 October as we go to Cyprus first for decompression. I had to leave slightly over a week or two before Teddy as I had made the decision to leave the Army and, as part of my termination, had to be back in the UK for a couple of months before I could do so. I was not too chuffed about that, but they were the rules of the game so I tried not to dwell on it too much.

The next operation was going to be our last of the tour. We boarded our newly arrived Mastiff vehicles. Windowless, apart from the windscreen, they were equipped with CCTV giving 180 degrees visibility so that those inside could see what was happening outside. They were equipped with seats and harnesses similar to those used in rally cars and were armed with .50 heavy machine guns up on the roof.

We arrived at FOB Inkerman without any problems or incidents and were shown to our accommodation, which consisted of a large tent fashioned from a parachute. Our cot beds were all pushed together, so you had to clamber in and out of bed at the top rather than the side. The nights were now extremely cold and we had to zip ourselves fully into our sleeping bags but, even so, I would wake up at about 2.00 or 3.00 am shivering. Even during the day, the temperature at midday was only reaching 30 degrees, a good 20 degrees colder than a few months before, which made our job a much easier.

We were patrolling with C Company out in the Jucelay area, which we had cleared previously during Operation LASTAY KULANG. The Taliban were trying to re-infiltrate the area, so we needed to keep them out. They were attacking day after day as they knew they needed to get rid of FOB Inkerman before they could move on to Sangin.

On one occasion, as we came back in from a patrol, we were just taking our armour off and sorting our kit out when we heard the enormous crack and a whoosh of an SPG-9, the same type of weapon that had killed Captain Hicks. As I mentioned previously, you hear the whoosh as it comes towards you and then the crack. This reminded us all that we were certainly not home and dry yet and that we had to keep on top of our game to avoid being wounded or killed.

By now, we were back to working in pairs, with one of us equipped with an SA80 and the other with a sniper rifle. Mo and Kingy paired up and, once again, Teddy and I were working for C Company together, with Teddy as my shooter. We patrolled out in Jucelay and Putay, providing support for C Company.

On our next patrol, we received intelligence that the Taliban were observing and following our troops in the area. It was decided to set a trap and the Sniper Platoon moved into a wadi where there were a considerable number of overhanging trees providing a lot of shadow in which we concealed ourselves. In the dark and looking out towards the light, we could observe everything very clearly while remaining unseen. We soon identified four Afghans equipped with farm tools who appeared to be tending some crops, while all around them were bundles of poppies. We set ourselves up and zapped each of them with the rangefinder. Each was assigned as a target to a sniper, Teddy and I being given the furthest on the right, at a range of around 400 metres away with no wind at all. Once we were ready, C Company moved off and carried on patrolling normally, leaving us watching and waiting. Shortly afterwards, we received a report over the radio that the four men had reported to their Taliban commander that the British were moving and asking him for orders. They had been told to pick up their weapons and follow C Company, which was going to be ambushed.

Sure enough, the four 'farm workers' dropped their tools, ran over to the bundles of poppies and pulled out AK-47s and RPGs. They then began to walk towards us, following C Company in order to attack them from the rear. Our safety catches came off and Fruity 'called' the ambush, 'On my count, 3 – 2 – 1. Fire!.' As soon as he uttered the word 'Fire!' there were four bullets in the air and four dead Taliban. It was the perfectly executed sniper ambush, with all four rifles firing simultaneously. We could not have done it better if we tried.

With that we withdrew and caught up with C Company, thereafter occupying a couple of compounds as it carried out big loop across our front but nothing further happened that day. I remember thinking it was somewhat surreal moving past the building where Teddy and I had been forced to spoon on the roof in order to stop from freezing to death on Operation LASTAY KULANG.

The next day we were out on patrol again and moving through an open. As we approached a group of buildings, we came under contact from the front and right. We took cover, manoeuvring ourselves into position to return fire, but the Taliban moved off in another direction. We continued patrolling and pushed through a dense and dark Green Zone area that was closer to Putay this time. We began to round a corner when Tom, who was behind us, came up on his PRR and reported that he had spotted an Afghan watching us and acting suspiciously. Just as he was being told to keep a sharp eye on the suspect, he came up on the air again and reported, 'Contact!.' That was all he had time to say because out of nowhere a group of Taliban jumped out of a building and opened fire with AK-47s. At the same time, another building to the right of us erupted as the enemy brought heavy fire down on us and launched one RPG at us, the air being filled with bullets and explosions cracking over our heads and all around us.

Teddy and I could not engage the enemy to our rear because Tom was in our way, returning fire, so concentrated on firing into the windows of the buildings to our right from where RPGs were being launched at us. Meanwhile, C Company had crossed the canal and was now pushing up the left-hand side of the buildings. After a while we were forced to cease fire to avoid the possibility of a blue-on-blue. Fruity told Teddy and me to cross the canal and stop half-way along from where C Company was advancing and try to put down some fire from there. He shouted for Donny and Jimmy to do the same as we started to crawl on our hands and knees towards C Company's position. The four of us waded through this canal with water up to our chests before clambering out on the other side. Bullets were zipping through trees, showering us with leaves and twigs, while the ground around us erupted in a storm of bullets. We slammed ourselves down at the forward edge of the tree line as C Company stormed into the attack. You could hear the grenades going off and the guys all shouting orders to each other as they pushed forward. We began firing at the muzzle flashes in windows and doorways while the rest of the Sniper Platoon moved in from the right, passing behind us and on towards our left. We ceased firing as C Company began clearing the buildings and by then there was further fire from the Taliban. It had been a close call, but at least we were still alive.

On the way back, we were up front and positioned ourselves up on some roofs to let C Company pass through, remaining there for a while to make sure that no Taliban was following up behind. Teddy and I had a last photograph taken of us on top of that roof, then jumped down and rejoined C Company as it headed back to FOB Inkerman. Back at base, we organised a team photograph of the entire sniper platoon. As I was standing there, a sergeant major came across and asked, 'Is Lance Corporal Cartwright here?' I went over to him and his words rang in my ears as he said, 'The next Chinook that comes in, you're on it and flying back home.' I closed my eyes and said, 'Thanks Sir.' I stood there with my head back and my eyes closed, facing the sky. I just thought, 'Thank God.'

I started to pack all my stuff away, all guys generally taking the piss as I got myself ready. We then sat around for a while. Tom had one of those Gucci little gizmos which played MP4s, so we had loads of episodes of *American Dad* and *Family Guy* which we all watched sitting inside our tent that night, which was a really good laugh and great for morale.

The next day Kingy and Mo and I were all ready to go with our kit packed when the Chinook came in. We moved down to the flight line and boarded the helicopter and, as it took off, it banked to the left and right and then, with nose dipped, flew off in the direction of Camp Bastion. We were going home. I will never ever forget that moment. I was in the rear of the aircraft, staring out of the tail gate at the ground passing below me thinking, 'That's it! I will never have to do this again. I made it out alive! I made it!.' Even now, whenever I see Chinooks I always think of that moment. The Bell Huey helicopters are synonymous with the Vietnam War, and the Harriers with the Falklands – for me, the Chinook will always evoke memories of Afghanistan and Helmand Province. I cannot describe my feelings during my final flight on that Chinook because it was such an immense moment in my life for which I struggle to find the words save to say, I was going home.

Epilogue

fter getting cleaned up and handing in all our weapons and ammunition, it was finally time to head home. On the way though, we stopped over in Cyprus to do our compulsory decompression where we could unwind, relax in civilian clothing, drink beer and eat barbecue food. The officer in charge of the decompression was great. He had us all lined up on parade, in our fresh new uniforms with which we had been issued before flying home. He stood on a small wall and said, 'Any man whom I catch in uniform half an hour after this parade will be charged. Is that understood?.' We all laughed and this kind of jokey comment really set the mood for what was to come over the next 48 hours. Buses arrived to ferry us down to the beach where we stayed all day. There was a trampoline in the sea floating on a giant rubber ring, sea canoes, and ice creams. It was a world apart considering that, only three days ago, I had been caught up in an ambush with a lot of the other guys around me. That night there was a big barbecue and ice cold beer while we were entertained by four stand-up comedians. They were so funny and it was such a great relief to just be laughing non-stop for ages.

The next morning was a little bit more formal. We were still in civilian clothing but we had to sit and watch videos and listen to briefings about adjusting back into life at home. We were constantly reminded of the fact that it was normal to have nightmares, and things would seem odd and boring. We were all congratulated and a video montage was shown of various pictures and films of the tour. After this, though, it was business as usual and we put our uniforms back on and boarded the buses for Akrotiri from where we took off for the UK and RAF Brize Norton.

We landed quite late. I think it was about 11.00 pm. As usual, we were herded like sheep to collect our baggage and wander through to the outside world and the old familiar October chill in the air, and the smell of freshly fallen rain. I had not seen rain for nearly three months. I loaded my bergen and holdall into the coach's cargo hold and presented my ID card to one of the admin clerks who ticked me off the list. Someone from the quartermaster's store handed me a bottle of ale that had been brewed especially for our welcome home. It was called "1759, welcome home edition". The label said it had been brewed by Red Rat brewery in Suffolk, and also had a comment on the back which read: 'Well done…from some Bergh Apton supporters! Mrs Alison Freeman.' It tasted great and I have kept the bottle.

On arriving at Elizabeth Barracks, the first thing I did was go to my car. Chris Worsley had asked me for a lift back to Peterborough so I waited for him outside of D Company lines. When we got back to my car I put the key in the ignition and turned but nothing happened. I could not believe it. I was absolutely livid. Mind you though, it had not been driven for three months, so I really should not have been surprised. The barrack guard Land Rover was driving about and stopped as it came by us . The driver opened the window and asked us if we needed some jump leads. The guard had anticipated this, bless him, and had spent the night driving around helping stranded soldiers. After a good zap of power my car burst into action and so Chris and I were now good to go back to Peterborough.

I had cocked up the timings when I told Annie what time I would be home. I said that I should be home around midnight. It was just after 3.00 am when I dropped Chris off and going on for 4.00 am when I pulled into my drive. She had said that she would wait up, but I doubted that she would last until that late. I opened the front door and walked into my dark flat. The living room light was on and there was Annie asleep on the sofa. I knelt down beside her and stroked her hair. As she stirred the blanket that was covering her slipped down to reveal a basque and stockings. I could not help but laugh and grin at the surprise she had planned for me. At that moment, she woke up and gave me the biggest hug I have ever had.

The next two weeks were much the same as R & R, just spent

enjoying myself and seeing everybody again. In any case, I still had Teddy and the rest of the guys in the back of my mind as they were still out in Afghanistan. I drove back to barracks to welcome B Company home and to start the ball rolling on my leaving the Army. There never were one or two specific reasons why I left the Royal Anglians. There were loads of little ones really. Sergeant Major Snow called me into his office one day and said it was great having me as a soldier under his command and, if I wanted back in, then I should give him a call. The RSM, WO1 Robinson, said the same and added that he would have me back in the unit in no time. So, knowing I had the Army as my safety net, I drove out of Elizabeth Barracks for the last time to start my life as a civilian.

I proposed to Annie in Paris just like I planned. She said yes which is also what I had planned so all was going well so far. But then something we had not planned happened: Annie fell pregnant. Just as I started working as a civilian, in a suit, in an office, I was also to become a father. I embraced it and did not shy away from it. I was happy to be a Dad, I felt ready. But it started to feel like I was living someone else's life. My life just felt it had a part missing. I was bored a lot of the time. I missed that rush of adrenaline. I used to drive at speed up to a roundabout and try my hardest not to brake but instead time the flow of traffic and slot into it just for fun. Work was interesting enough, I had never really worked within an environment with women, and so was scared and unsure as to what to say to them. I did not want to look like a weirdo, but at the same time did not wish to seem as though I was trying to pull them either.

In addition, the mentality of my colleagues was so different. In the Royal Anglians I knew that every man there would risk his life for me and I would do likewise, but I would not trust the men in the office with my biro. There was so much back stabbing, along with immaturity and over-inflated egos. I made friends with a guy called Phil Dedman who really listened to me and was genuinely interested in my tour of Helmand. However, I did not like the job that much and wanted out. I did not have to wait long because the recession kicked in, and being in sales for the first time ever was made near damn impossible for me. Even the more seasoned sales people struggled to hit targets. I was trying to sell search engine optimisation, which is basically a service that places your website on the front page of Google in response to any search phrase for which you want to be found. It is a really good form of advertising but it comes at a big cost and, with businesses tightening their belts, I was doomed. After three months of being a civilian I was now unemployed, and with a baby on the way and buying a new house I thought I would have to rejoin the Army.

A good friend of mine, Dave Phillips, managed to get me a job working as a van driver for the property maintenance firm for which he worked. I would drop a decorator off at his job, pick up the bathroom suites from the depot, deliver them to the plumbers, pick up the old suites and dispose of them at the depot. The firm had a contract with Mears who were renovating the kitchens and bathrooms of all the council houses in Peterborough so the job seemed secure. I loved being a white van man with my long hair now there was no sergeant major to tell me to get it cut. But it did not last. The boss kept increasing my workload so the pressure increased.

My baby daughter, Sophie, was born on 3 July, so the sleepless nights started. One day, whilst driving along the A47 in Peterborough, I was behind a big old articulated lorry when suddenly, out of nowhere, a stone flew off the top of the trailer in front and came crashing into my windscreen. I yelled, 'Contact!' at the top of my voice and once again heard the rattle of gunfire and the whooshes of RPGs. The smell of cordite burned my nose and smoke grenades clawed at my throat. I then remembered I was not in Helmand but in my van. When I arrived at the depot, I climbed out and chain-smoked about three cigarettes while my hands trembled and my stomach was in knots.

After that I could not sleep at all. I saw silhouettes of people in the corner of my eye. I felt unsafe in crowded areas and that eventually grew to whenever I was outside. Annie told me that maybe I should seek help, and that there was nothing wrong with that. I remembered the briefings at Cyprus and finally agreed to go to my GP. He diagnosed post traumatic stress disorder (PTSD) for which I underwent six weeks of counselling, which really helped. My counsellor recommended that maybe I should write things down. However, I found it easier to talk so I recorded my voice instead. I spoke as if I was in the pub telling someone what had happened on my tour and I felt better.

But then the worst thing of all happened. After moving into our new home, irregularities started appearing in my paycheck. Some times I was not paid. This carried on through Christmas and into January. The excuse was that Mears had not processed the invoices correctly. In reality I was working for someone who played God by deciding who would be paid and who would not so they could keep our wages to clear their own personal debts. I walked out in February. I had a child and a mortgage, but no income and was owed over £2,000 in unpaid wages.

'Welcome to civilian life,' I thought as I stood in the dole queue, 'What has happened to me?.' I felt stripped of all my dignity. I had fought for this country twice, so maybe it was time to get something back from it. It took a few hours and then a few letters and telephone calls before I received any dole. The job centre could not find any record of me paying any National Insurance and initially claimed that I was not entitled to anything. I soon proved them wrong when I showed them my pay slips from the Army. I also tried to back-date my claim to when I actually left my last job but this was refused. I explained that I had tried finding a job off my own back but that apparently was not a good enough reason. I needed to find a job as soon as possible as, by this time, I was receiving letters from companies threatening legal action and bailiffs.

I started my own legal proceedings to obtain my unpaid wages. In the meantime I contacted SSAFA, the Soldiers Sailors and Air Force Association, which is a charity exclusively for the armed forces. Pam from SSAFA obtained help for us from the Royal British Legion and the Royal Anglian Association. I spoke to Jay who was now working as the recruiting sergeant for Peterborough. He told me he could get me back into the Royal Anglians in no time. I thought hard about that and, in the end, it was my brother who talked me round. He said he could not let me rejoin the infantry to be killed, and then have to look my daughter in the eye and tell her he did not do everything he could to stop me. He was right, my priorities had changed. I could no longer be how I used to be and go off to wherever the Army sent me. I had to stay and look after my family, but also have a military job. That's when it hit me. I knew of part of the Army that provides armed security in the UK. It never goes abroad and works shifts. My next-door neighbour, Rick, has a brother in it and he told me all I needed to know. I phoned the careers office and, in less than four months, I was starting my second career in the Army in the MPGS, Military Provost Guard Service.

I eventually received my unpaid wages through the county court ten months after I walked out. All my belongings are still mine and not the bailiffs.' I am employed in a familiar job but it has to be said a lot calmer version of it. Finally, after a year of being a civilian and nearly wrecking my life, my feet are back on the ground. I have my family and my life to look forward to.

When I think back to my time in Helmand, I remember the good as well as the bad things. Like when you have a tattoo, you know it hurts a little while you are having it done but you cannot remember exactly how much it hurts until you're back in the chair having another. I know that physically and mentally Afghanistan was very hard on me and every other soldier who fought in Op HERRICK 6 but I doubt I will ever again truly appreciate just how hard it was. Now, though, when I read or watch something about the First or Second World War, and any other conflict in the twentieth or twenty-first century, I feel a lot closer to those people who fought in them. I know from first-hand experience what it feels like to be there waiting to launch into battle. To be shot at, and to shoot at someone. To hear the sound of incoming mortar bombs and cries of 'Man down!' and worry whether it is a close friend. Instead of feeling worry or apprehensive when I recall the summer of 2007, I now embrace it and accept that it is just part of my life history.